7322

Albuquerque Academy

D0044207

False Prophets in the Fiction of
Camus, Dostoevsky, Melville, and Others

False Prophets

in the Fiction of
Camus, Dostoevsky, Melville,
and Others

By

Felix S. A. Rysten

UNIVERSITY OF MIAMI PRESS

Coral Gables, Florida

Copyright © 1972 by
University of Miami Press
Library of Congress Catalog Card Number 77–158928
ISBN 0–87024–226–1

All rights reserved, including rights of reproduction and use in any
form or by any means, including the making of copies by any photo
process, or by any electronic or mechanical device, printed or
written or oral, or recording for sound or visual reproduction or for
use in any knowledge or retrieval system or device, unless
permission in writing is obtained from the copyright proprietors.

Manufactured in the United States of America

Permissions to quote excerpts from the writings of Albert Camus
were generously granted by Albert A. Knopf, Inc. for material from
The Fall, © 1956; *Caligula and Three Other Plays*, © 1958;
and *The Rebel*, © 1956.

808.83
Rys

To Diana

Albuquerque Academy

17322

Contents

Preface

THIS BOOK, IN ITS INITIAL PREPARATION, WAS THE doctoral dissertation which I submitted in 1968 to the University of Southern California for a degree in Comparative Literature. I wrote that first manuscript after it had occurred to me that certain novels had in common a main character who could be said to be a spokesman of doom, a self-appointed leader insisting on an exodus from (illusory) bondage toward a promising change, a satanic messiah proclaiming the way to a false security. For me, having started with this premise, a biblical parody seemed evident. Since a clear example of this literary trend would be Albert Camus' *The Fall*, I concentrated, once I began writing, on the reason for such a framework and on the Christian implication of such a design. This approach next led me to consider Camus' models: the works of Franz Kafka and André Malraux, of Fyodor Dostoevsky and Herman Melville. It has seemed to me that these authors in their fiction reflect upon the common theme that within our Western cultural system there is a severe discontentment with our earthbound aspirations. I have analyzed this idea, this leitmotif that man's distress seeks a relief through nervous impatience for a transcendent mystery. Even when God is denied Being, man wills to escape into an ideal, whatever its form. It is my contention that *The Fall, The Possessed,* and *Moby-Dick* depict hollow leaders who capitalize on man's desperate need to place his faith in something, in anything which promises release from monotony, from confinement, from fear of obliteration. These self-appointed prophets are false because they engage man's willingness to slide into instantaneous salvation for their own selfish ends. Within the fictional work where they operate they have an air of reality. However, for the reader they are intended as mirrors of anarchy in which his conscience is given a warning —a warning that not only does salvation lie in a future and hierarchic unity, but that it is already within reach at the time of each man's earthly life.

To wrest meaning from an apparently futile existence and to usurp the traditionally divine right to grant happiness after death, Camus has advocated hope in the solidarity of man, suggesting that at the root of chaos lies each man's indecision to unite in the common purpose of *this* life. Malraux has insisted on man's duty to match his power in contest with the annihilating forces that surround him in order to find fulfillment in resistance to death's inevitability. Kafka has proposed salvation in unflinching and honest awareness of the unavoidable elimination that awaits each man. Their great predecessors, Dostoevsky and Melville, have resolved that in the end goodness, as divine manifestation on earth, would eventually triumph, and that man can only hope for happiness in obedience to God's commandments. Considering these premises, I have ascertained that, according to the authors I have discussed, there is a genre in fiction which, expressed by dramatic methods, can be called the tragic enactment of our ominous age.

In having written this book, I am appreciative of the helpful suggestions given to me by Professors R. Bellé and A. Armato when the manuscript was in the process of becoming. My appreciation is also extended to the members of the University of Southern California libraries without whose goodwill the necessity of research might well have led into a maze with unmarked exits.

Above all, in the writing of this book, as in many other respects, I greatly value that I have been among the Comparative

Literature students at the University of Southern California who owe much to the knowledge, awareness, and affectionate concern of Professor Norma L. Goodrich.

False Prophets in the Fiction of
Camus, Dostoevsky, Melville, and Others

1

Introduction

To READ THE FICTION WRITTEN IN THE PAST HUNDRED years is to be shown a territory charted by novelists for the use of a society wildly seeking a direction. Writers in general have felt the need to define, within their fictional worlds, certain fantastic boundaries within which man can govern himself. The artistic reality of these *terrae cognitae* is a reflection on the private and collective responsibility of their inhabitants. Often it pictures an ideal perverted by a society, by a group which turns a well-defined realm into a maze from which each man struggles to escape. Within this labyrinth man has a doubt in the justness of his (false) confinement, a doubt in his ability to define himself according to imposed limits. Rejecting man-made restrictions, he loses his control, next his perspective, and thus his ability to define himself in terms of others, in relation to any limit of self-perfectibility or the ultimate limit of a transcendent aspiration. In eager escape man flees into a limitlessness in which he will be annihilated from without or from within, his freedom having become the right to destroy for personal salvation. It seems, for example, that some of the most violently pessimistic observations of this nature made during the last decades can be found in Louis-Ferdinand Céline's *Journey to the End of Night* (1932). This does not prove that

Céline's novel is representative of an age, but it does suggest that the fictional reality concentrates on the same somber attitude of destructive anarchy which had already been stated dramatically by such previous masters as Fyodor Dostoevsky, or Herman Melville, both remarkable for their moments of gloom. It further seems likely that Céline portrays, with a vengeance, the horrors of violence which other modern novelists such as Albert Camus, André Malraux, and Franz Kafka have developed unforgettably in their masterpieces.

Since the middle of the last century the Christian religion of the West and, in fact, the Christian cultural system in general have been under attack by such writers as Fyodor Dostoevsky, Friedrich Nietzsche, Jean-Paul Sartre, and Albert Camus in a constant process of ever-accelerating reevaluation. God, first undermined, then dethroned, was eventually, and by such novelists as Dostoevsky, Melville, Malraux, and Camus, replaced by the man-god, by the sovereign self within each man's being. Yet, if concern with nonphysical reality is considered to be not only a state of ultimate importance, but also a questioning awareness of one's existence, then a Céline as well as a Paul Tillich can be termed a religious figure. These two writers, a blasphemer and an essentially Christian advocate, have created the extremes between which, in fiction, philosophical attitudes fluctuate—attitudes which speculate on the possibility of "otherness."

Man, in the modern world of the last hundred years, finds himself alone in the universe, without a god, without a rational system to guide him, in short, without an identifiable order. Modern spokesmen such as Camus, Malraux, and Kafka discuss this theme of isolation and its implications by starting with the concept of "the absurd" to define man and his relationship with the world at large. Since Western man has lived for hundreds of years within a predominantly Christian civilization, it can be said that the philosophical concept of "the absurd" is peculiar to this cultural system, this generally recognizable frame of reference for thought and for action. Works written within a Christian framework tend to concentrate upon man's separation from God or upon his natural state after Adam's fall from communion with the Father. The search of the author, of the character, and possibly of the reader has generally represented a quest for a closer union with mankind and a desire to know a transcendent mystery. In the narratives which employ religious types and images, there is a given reality, identifiable as a Christian background, against which the search for the meaning of life is depicted. It is from the observation of this reality that the concept of "the absurd" was understood.

Although in a consideration of the relationship between man and a certain literary work there is the danger of a certain subjectivity, still, since the function of art is creation, fiction can be said to aspire toward the infinite and the reader may therefore assume that the vision conjured up in his mind is, to some large degree, indicative of the artist's intent; thus, he is granted an insight into his own esthetic experience. Fortunately, the author has imposed a limitation, which allows for an accepted standard of objectivity. The restrictive factor is ordained by the words used as, for instance, the manner in which the characters attempt to express themselves. Therefore the reader can aspire toward becoming one with the elusive world of the characters so long as he respects the author's timely rationalization of fleeting or static reality. In this manner it is possible to identify with the image of a character portrayed in the process of estrangement. Bringing the vision into focus, we are reacting according to the author's intent.

The frequently observed estrangement of fictional characters can be brought about either by society's judgment or by their own rejection of its judges. In the latter case, the fictional people go into a self-imposed exile because of disappointments which resulted from a misplaced faith. They cut themselves off when they have defined the source of their discouragement. Disenchanted, they gather strength by resenting the random forces which destroyed their beliefs. This strength they project unto those who are still without conviction. These undecided, fictional persons, soon converted, turn into men "possessed" by their misleaders; and, although they can recognize their guides as imposters, these ready followers prefer the surface security to a painful *demasqué*. The reader can recognize the author's terrible intent, and it is for him to acknowledge the hypocrisy which brought about the terrible vision of false salvation.

In novels such as Camus' *The Fall*, Dostoevsky's *The Possessed*, and Melville's *Moby-Dick* there appears to be an obvious purpose to show the fate of those who place their trust in misleadership. Apparently, the esthetic experience, in confrontation with these novels, is, in part, determined by the relationship of content and form. Both Dostoevsky and Melville turned the novel to the uses of tragedy, and adapted this classical form. Camus learned from these predecessors and understood, as they did, that the reader should be given the chance to act the play rather than to contemplate it. The reader is therefore drawn into the moving drama and made to live the experience. This employment of dramatic method is highly suited to the depiction of prophetic characters. These pseudo-inheritors of divine unity require a light and a pedestal, as well as the strength to lure scattered disbelievers in Christian salvation.

The semblance of unity which such novels offer serves a two-fold aim. Within the literary work of art, it creates a tension transmitted to the reader; and, moreover, the balanced, artistic presentation which suggests an ordered universe is contradicted by the chaos of the content. These three novels present an analysis of their time; they are a mirror in which the conscience of the reader is trapped.

The three novels, *The Fall*, *The Possessed*, and *Moby-Dick*, suggest a five-act classical tragedy. Within this world of tragic conflict destructive figures rule. *The Fall* is dominated by Jean-Baptiste Clamence, *The Possessed* by Nikolay Stavrogin, and *Moby-Dick* by Ahab. As principals they are portrayed like contemporary heroes of amoral actions, who destroy the people around them. They have been maimed by a chance encounter, so that it seems imperative for them to assert their own significance via a personal revenge upon an indifferent unknown. In this obsession they require the presence of people with whom they can fill their own world of hatred. They require a following of ordinary men to enhance their stature and to relieve the loneliness of their demonic mission. In order to attract allies for their treacherous pursuit against the established, universal order, they must come disguised as leaders touched by the

spark of insight. Their powerful appearance hides a *paysage
démoralisé*, and, since they live on solitary heights, they are
admired by those who suffer from discontentment and a feeling
of loneliness. They proclaim to be the beginning and the end
of the recognition of man's complicity in the existing world of
anarchy. Since in their worlds a state of anarchy is the only
identifiable norm left, people flock toward them in recognition
of the familiar. It is essential for these misleaders that they
maintain their strength through indifference. They have attempted to love as an escape from their violent mission of
judgment, but they left love behind them when they discarded
their innocent belief that the universe was essentially good.
They reject everything which binds man to man and all that
can serve as go-between for themselves and the Creation. Having considered any human quality and any man-created inven-
tion as an intolerable deception of harmonious existence, they
must retreat to a *malconfort* of isolation, doubt, and fear. In
personal agony they will disintegrate in the void of their own
dissent.

Already before their fall into awareness, they had set themselves above others; after their fall they continue to do the
same. Lucidity has shown them the way out of their blessed
contentment, and in their newly acquired perception they assume that mankind will be served by their brand of nihilism.
They have one, sole certainty: having understood what they
believe to have been the irresponsibility of their earlier ideals,
they have become converted to a belief in absolute dictatorship.
Cut off from the cosmos in the prison of civilization, they are
the epitome of dissatisfaction with God and with life; they
must suffer the woe of those "through whom temptation
cometh." They tempt their followers into acknowledging their
reality by proposing a solidarity based on the fear of refusal to
follow a savior. They remember that suffering is the natural
condition of man in an evil world, and in this knowledge they
occupy an eminent position—a standing which needs to be
preserved so that they will not perish in the judgment of the
world. Like Cain, they make themselves judges of God's deeds
and thereby of His Creation. By having appointed themselves
as godheads in their own established realms, they turn the per-

sons whom they have converted into emanations of their own evil spirit; and so they are fated to bring to a close the reign of uncertain disbelief, the reign which slowly but unsurely tries to dehumanize man.

2

A Literary Climate
1860-1960

WHEN, IN 1932, LOUIS-FERDINAND CÉLINE SENT HIS
fictional double on a journey to the end of night, he warned:

> Remember this well Ferdinand, that the beginning of the end is
> a loss of a sense of proportion. . . . It began with a wild lack of
> moderation! Foreign frenzies! An outworn sense of fitness, an
> end to strength! It was written. Chaos for all then? Why not?
> For everyone? It is agreed. We are not going in that direction,
> we are rushing there—It's a real rout. I've seen the soul, Fer-
> dinand, give way, bit by bit, lose its balance and dissolve in the
> vast welter of apocalyptic ambition. It began in 1900. . . . From
> that time onwards . . . each strove to see who could immolate
> himself the soonest to the monster of no heart and no restraint.
> . . . What is this monster? A great brute tumbling along
> wherever it listeth! Its wars and its drooling flood in towards us
> already from all sides. We shall be swept away on this tide—
> yes, swept away.[1]

With this desperate realization the author has expressed an
awareness which is often found in twentieth-century literature.
Of course, it can be said that Céline's Muse suffers from bitter
disillusion after a night of despair, but it is nevertheless true
that with the theme of chaos, writers of our time have been
frequently occupied. Vague terms like "sense of doom" and
"loss of proportion" do not cover any ideas peculiar to our age.

This perception of life as expressed by artists can be traced back to Romanticism, although with this distinction that in the intervening years the veil of beauty has been tattered to expose the ugly content.

Already in Byron's poem "Darkness" (1816) there has been described the dream of the loveless world destroyed in a fiery holocaust, and, like the man in Shelley's sonnet "Lift Not the Painted Veil" (1824), artists have discovered "the chasm, sightless and drear." Man, alone in his space-time continuum, has known for some time that none of his subjective strivings can influence the universe. He is a part of Nature, and yet Nature is indifferent to his mood and yearning. He is a victim of time, cut off from the divine source, having only the certainty of death. While certain writers of the Romantic era still saw an aspect of the divine reflected in Nature, the authors of today can only turn to the self for inspiration. The proof of God's presence, as in Samuel Beckett's *Waiting for Godot* (1952), has been reduced to the precarious certainty that for waiting man He will come the day after today. Nevertheless, modern writers, even as they reject the promise of God, struggle with the religious problem—but the God they evoke is structured in negative argument. Sometimes they indulge, like Céline, in blasphemous argument with the Creator and His Creation. But in either case, the search for a god remains, in Marcel Arland's apt words, "the eternal torment of man, whether he insists on creating him or destroying him."[2] Friedrich Nietzsche found Him dead, as he first stated in *The Joyful Wisdom* (1882);[3] still, the "religious" impulse persists. The quest for the transcendent that is beyond all reason and beyond all proof has not ended; but God remains invisible and unknowable. The writer, therefore, in trying to approach the unknown, is limited to the universe of human experience and restricted by the realm of the mind and the senses that work from the visible world.

The way a writer responds to the challenge of existence and interprets the nature of man may depend upon his knowledge of the absence of God. But, as Paul Tillich states the problem: "Whatever the subject matter which an artist chooses . . . he cannot escape religion even if he rejects religion, for religion is the state of being ultimately concerned. And in every style the ultimate concern of a human group is manifest."[4] If this is so, then even a negative reflection of life, and in its extreme case the emergence of the demonic, are essentially religious in their confrontation of reality. All that matters is the degree of honesty with which the writer interprets life. The questioning of external phenomena may dissolve in skepticism or atheism; however, the act of inquiry shows apprehension and implies that life is not unconditionally accepted. Without questioning religion could hardly exist: religion means awareness of life and a search for what is beyond the horizon of human experience. Thus, although Céline on the one hand and Tillich on the other begin with opposing premises and different forms of expression, they arrive at substantially the same conclusion.

This is the challenge which confronts the modern artist: how to question life when the direction to the beyond is not given, or, in other words, how to give meaning to a universe that is indifferent to man's plight and which, to all appearances, is without the presence of God. Man confronts an existence which seems to be inexplicably futile, and yet he is to make a separate peace in a world of futility. He prefers to deny the desire to merge with the beyond—this fatuous yearning for an Absolute —still he must quest for his identity. If he gives up this search, he becomes an empty self in which he perishes. This is not to say that those who seek on find the way to their identity: the most they can expect is to find a self-awareness in the reality of defiance of death.

In the quest the modern writer looks within and finds no entity that he can define as the self, no ever-fixed mark by which he can evaluate his experiences. Yet the writer must somehow come to terms with the times in order not to be swept away. He can create an artistic moment in which he and others also may find an understanding of themselves and their world. He can develop a value system which may suggest an identifiable order, a point of reference, an instant of stability to consider the stilling of unrest.

Albert Camus has spoken of the stone in *The Myth of Sisyphus* (1942) to suggest a characteristic of the world in which man moves; he makes it a symbol of the burden man carries, as well as of the silent indifference of man's surroundings. Traveling through Italy as a young adult, Camus saw the painting "The Flagellation" by Pierro della Francesca. He was astonished by the detachment, the superior indifference which the attitudes of both Christ and the tormentor convey, and observed that their faces were stilled, were forever free of "la malédiction de l'esprit."[5] It is the same indifference which characterizes man when he identifies with the stone and does not seek refuge in hope. In this acceptance man acknowledges a sterile liberation, a liberation which delivers him to the eternal present of the physical experience. However, this physical experience carries its own seed of destruction. When it exists, it denies itself in confrontation with suffering and the resultant awareness of death. Fear spurs man on to question his reason for being, but no answer is ever given. Man discovers that there is no definable correspondence between him and his world and in this recognition of lack of relationship man discovers what Camus has called the "absurd."

This theory of absurdity describes the position of man within his world as a dialogue with a silent partner. Without reassurance that the answer man has provided himself is correct, he becomes estranged from a world which appeared to belong to him. Man begins as part of a whole, but ends alone. In Camus' words: "I was born poor, but under a happy sky, into a natural world of harmony, not one of hostility. Therefore, I have begun within a fullness, not within a disharmony."[6] Absurdity is disturbed harmony, undermined stability, and broken unity. It consists of harmony and disruption, instability and equilibrium, just as indifference is formed out of meaning and meaninglessness. Both Meursault, the main character of *The Stranger* (1942), and Clamence, the compulsive talker of *The Fall* (1956), experience an initial harmony with the world until a conflict exposes the meaninglessness of their world. From the displacement of familiar perception and the remembrance of the way it was, the absurd is born. This drama of the silent world against unity-demanding man can be enacted everywhere. The disgust of Roquentin in Jean-Paul Sartre's *Nausea* (1938), when he is confronted with the suffocating fullness of the universe, is as much an example of it as the silent stone which, in its massiveness, resists identification.

Once the absurd has shaken man's world, he will want to turn to some *one* because some *thing* does not answer. In Camus' definition the other one, with whom the terror can be shared, is not to be found and man's estrangement deepens. The absence of the other one is never clearly presented, and the possibility for communication is not denied. The other is simply not there when needed. This philosophic principle of absurdity is not restricted to Camus. It can also be found in the fictional world of André Malraux, although here the term "absurd" is not so much a deliberate choice of reference as an incidental observation. Malraux imparted to his generation "absurdity" as a characteristic of reality. In his epistolary novel *The Temptation of the West* (1926), Malraux introduced into the thought of Europe this notion which, later, Camus developed into a premise for awareness and action. "At the core of Western civilization," said Malraux through a fictional correspondent in a letter to his friend, "there is a hopeless contradiction, in whatever shape we discover it: that between man and what he has created. . . . This spirit of contradiction trains our consciousness to give way and prepares us for the metallic realms of the absurd."[7] Malraux, writing in the wake of World War I, realized that Western civilization was disintegrating, and in this novel he conveyed the feeling of despair and absurdity.

In an absurd universe of disassociated realities Malraux found a twofold resource: courage and action, metaphysical and physical courage of a boldly hopeless kind, taking the form of adventure, with the self as stake in perilous circumstances. The encounter is to have one purpose: the sense of living derived from defiance of death. Out of Malraux' experience in China came *The Conquerors* (1928). Garine, the main character of this novel, has experienced the absurd. There is a kinship between him and Meursault. He too has to sit through a trial in which the absurdity of human existence becomes manifest, and he too experiences it as a kind of comedy which is played around him. The judges try his stand-in, not him, even though this stand-in carries his name. Equally apparent, however, are the differences between Garine and Meursault. Meursault has been an amateur all his life, never fully committed to any action. During the trial Garine only pretends to be uninvolved, and so he discovers the gap between him and society; he committed his crime—financial assistance to women who could not pay for an abortion—in anarchistic conviction. Meursault discovers in the trial the absurdity of an existence which practices a senseless ritual. Garine discovers the same, but he fights back and goes to China to join the Communist party even though he does not find that this justifies his existence. Meursault and Garine undergo the same confrontation; for one it is the end, for the other the beginning. Camus noted that *The Stranger* was meant as "an exercise in objectivity and detachment."[8] Malraux told Trotzky that *The Conquerors* is "first of all an accusation of the human condition."[9]

For Camus absurdity is the foreground, for Malraux it is background. Meursault's trial and its aftermath take up half the narrative. Garine's trial is sketched in to explain his present life in China and its end. Garine says: "You may live believing in the vanity of all things, but you cannot live in that vanity."[10] Malraux' *The Conquerors* is the commentary on this remark, because it describes the struggle of Garine against the absurd forces of the world. In *The Stranger* absurdity indicates lack of meaning for a satisfactory relation between man and his world. While in *The Conquerors* absurdity may have the same meaning as in *The Stranger*, the consciousness of human experience only considers it as part of the cause. Absurdity is here related to the fact that man is threatened by forces against which he cannot defend himself, but which dignity tells him he must boldly face.

These forces which man finds within himself, or which he finds opposing him from the outside, inspire as well as threaten. In Malraux's *The Royal Way* (1930) this is even clearer than in *The Conquerors*. A young man, Claude, journeys into the jungle with his older friend, Perken. Claude finds the absurd, symbolized by the wilderness, inspiring; he hopes to find there gigantic Siamese figures. As fictional experience this novel is an obsession because of the curious mixture of chance and danger the trip involves. There is the chance for Claude to obtain statues and for Perken to make money, and for both the danger of death within the land of insects and hostile tribes. Perken and his companion are the successors of Garine and his name-less friend, the narrator of the novel. Just as *The Conquerors* ends with the illness of Garine, which will be followed by a certain death, the final page of *The Royal Way* describes Per-ken's dying. Their end is absurd, but from absurdity they drew the strength to fight as men.

Symbol of the dehumanizing power of the absurd—the jungle—is Grabot, who is initially only identified as the man who went into the wilderness and did not come back. Eventu-ally they find him, eyeless and tied to a millstone; he is no longer human; he has become the heart of darkness. The most desperate situation occurs when the absurdity becomes so powerful that human existence disappears. Grabot has dis-solved in the wilderness. He is the abyss which Claude and Perken discover, the abyss into which they, too, can fall. He is similar to the terrorist Hong who stands with Garine, the man who more resembles Garine than any of his party members. Garine continues to say, aware of the paradox, that he fights to give others a meaningful existence, while Hong, in his an-archistic activities, only avenges a miserable past. With the figures of Hong and Grabot, "negative" doubles of Garine and Perken, the limit of existence is touched: absurdity cancels out all human aspects. The heat of battle in which man defends himself against the absurd powers has made way for the chill of madness in which inhuman powers have triumphed.

Novelists like Camus and Malraux describe terror, and in this regard they may be called literary descendants of Franz Kafka. In Camus' *récits* murder, suicide, and annihilation are common occurrences. In Malraux' novels characters are always fighting; in *The Trial* (1925) and *The Castle* (1926) the K.'s are continually menaced. All these manifestations of violence signify the flood which is to sweep man away, but the meaning of battle, murder, and threat is peculiar to each author. In the fiction of Camus and Malraux this meaning can perhaps be ex-plained in reference to a given character; in Kafka's work this is impossible. In *The Conquerors* the battle is meaningful be-cause it temporarily brings Garine loss of his loneliness, while Martha, in *The Misunderstanding* (1945), has gone on a mur-dering rampage to secure a carefree life. There nevertheless

exists the question of whether the illusions of Martha and
Garine can support the meaning of their actions. Their deeds
may be justifiable to themselves, but they are eventually to be
judged by an outside norm which may reveal to them the absurdity of action. In this regard it is important to note that in
the three works which are fundamental to the concept of the
absurd—*The Stranger, The Conquerors,* and *The Trial*—court
trials play an important part in which the individual case is
inspected with general rule. After the trial Meursault and
Garine suddenly realize that life is absurd, that is, they acknowledge the discrepancy between the world and the way they
had perceived the world to be. Their misdeed has been given
a significance which it does not have for them. The life of
Joseph K., surrounded by invisible judges, only slowly becomes absurd. His (mis-)deeds are being given an importance
which is beyond his comprehension.

It is characteristic of works that deal with the absurd to discuss right and wrong in doubtful terms and to depict the hero
as not knowing how he has offended the common norm. The
narratives of Kafka often begin with a puzzling occurrence
which confronts a character. In the works of Camus there is
shown a break in the known scheme of ordinary experience, a
disruption which the characters cannot ignore. And in Malraux'
novels people fight to discover the meaning behind their daily
existence.

In absurdity meaning is questionable. A desirable, general
norm which can be used as guiding light is conspicuously absent. Each man searches alone. Another characteristic, then, of
absurdity which pertains to Kafka, as well as to Camus and
Malraux, is the isolation of the individual. Man has to rely on
something he shares with others—Kafka: the judges, Camus:
daily experience, Malraux: the fight—and when he is unsuc-
cessful, his situation has become absurd. He needs a map, but
he has to do without. He must journey according to plan, but
he lacks a compass. If he fails to become oriented, he will
cease to exist. As the necessity for the search increases, his
situation will become more desperate and his isolation will in-
crease. Camus says in *The Myth of Sisyphus* that man asks for

meaning but that the universe remains silent. In other words, man needs a plan for which he asks in vain.

This discrepancy between the need for and the absence of a sense of direction, which isolates man, finds its esthetic expression in the novels of Camus, Malraux, and Kafka. In *The Stranger* the reader is drawn into an absurd experience as a result of Meursault's reactions. The *récit* is a monologue of someone who describes himself and his deeds, and yet fails to create a picture of his personality. The reader listens to the story of Meursault's life without being able to give meaning to the character's actions; he tries to become oriented but is denied the possibility. The work of Malraux, on the other hand, is a defense against absurdity. If Camus' reader became isolated because he was incapable of identifying himself with the character, Malraux' reader is cut off in his confrontation with the forces of death and suffering. On the one hand, these forces prevent man from getting oriented—the work of Malraux contains several "lost" souls like Tchen, Hong, and Grabot— on the other, these forces compel man to resist and defend himself. It is true that with Malraux man lives to his full potential only when he pitches himself against suffering; he truly *is* when he exists by the grace of what will eliminate him. "And death is always there," says Perken to Claude, "like a standing proof of the futility of life." And, Perken goes on: "What weighs on me is—how shall I put it?—my human lot, my limitations; that I must grow old, and time, that loathsome thing, spread through me like a cancer, inevitably. Time— there you have it."[11] Malraux, as expected, compares absurdity with a cancer and considers the forces which threaten man and his fragile individuality as absurd.

As Malraux develops as novelist, the frequency of the concept of the absurd diminishes. A new emphasis is placed on action, rather than on the deed which leads to broken unity. The intrigue in *Man's Fate* (1933) and *Man's Hope* (1937) is determined by the struggle between man and the dehumanizing forces which attack his human existence. The novels are a call to solidarity, and with Kyo and Manuel and their resistance one can identify. These heroes exist because of the conflict, whether they fight with words, putting existence on trial, or do battle with a concrete enemy. A similar development can be traced in Camus, who also came to see the necessity of solidarity against suffering, man's mightiest opponent. Both authors had a growing awareness of mankind's need to reunite. Rieux and Claude were willing to find the meaning in life at the risk of losing the contest with the world's brute forces. With their survival at the end of the novels the authors affirm man's hope.

In the work of Kafka all the characteristics of the absurd can be found, while we hardly ever run across the word itself. Kafka, without any foregone solution, searches with his characters. It would be a tenuous position to hold that both the K.'s of The Trial and The Castle are in quest of the meaning of life. Tenuous because, first of all, they cannot allow themselves such a general search: one is looking for his accuser, the other for his employer; further because, with their effort to find their guilt and job, their existence is at stake. It is impossible for Kafka to say, with Camus, that there is no meaning, or be convinced with Malraux that man must find a counterbalance against the meaninglessness of life. Within the context of the novels the K.'s slowly lose their footing and constantly seek escape from the threat of nothingness. It cannot be maintained that they cannot become oriented, but it cannot be said either that they are able to do so. The labyrinthine novels of Kafka are monstrous orientation charts, as ingenious as they are incomplete. Man can wander there forever. He will always discover a new corridor and there find an unforeseen possibility. Every corridor, however, has a dead end, and so every possibility leads to at least one impossibility. Thus, man is not isolated, but in his journeys through the labyrinth his aloneness— slowly but unsurely—becomes a fact.[12] Joseph K. alienates himself from his surroundings the more he tries to find the reason for his guilt. In The Castle the whole village turns against K. when he tries to seek contact with his employer. That which affirms his being man is immediately denied; every denial of purpose and need creates the chance of a new approach, until at last the trap at dead center closes. All characteristics of Garine and Meursault, which are related to the absurd, were already present in Joseph K. The questions, Who is Joseph K.? and What did Joseph K. do?, return as echoes. If one wants to know, for example, if he is guilty, one is referred to the judges who, in their turn, refer back to the accused, a process infinitely repeated. The individuality of man is eliminated in favor of changing perspectives. The absurd here is the simultaneous yes and no, the repetitious ambivalence of the work itself. The reader who identifies with K. is drawn into a situation full of contradictions which force him to take a stand. With K. he hopes that Westwest is in the Castle and with Kafka that, having written about life's labyrinth, the course of existence has been charted. But he hopes in vain. In this manner the answer to the question, What is absurdity?, can be found in the experience within the reader's mind.

When man is forced to find his bearing and the opportunity to do so is lacking, he is in an absurd situation. From a religious point of view this absence of an orientation chart is related to the disappearance of Christianity as a "cultural system"; that is to say, as a generally accepted frame of reference for thought and action. There is rivalry between the Christian faith and the belief in the absurd. In *The Plague* (1947) and *The Stranger*, in *Man's Fate* and Fyodor Dostoevsky's *The Possessed* (1871–1872), the priest enters when the threat of death has become acute. Father Paneloux knows in the beginning of the novel why the plague makes people die. The confessor visits the condemned Meursault, and it is Tchen in Malraux' novel and Stavrogin in Dostoevsky's who carry on a conversation with a priest. When man is confronted with death and finds it difficult to approach a new enigma, priests offer them, in the form of Christian faith, a guiding line. In the work of Camus and Malraux, as well as in *The Possessed* or, for that matter, in *The Brothers Karamazov* (1879–1880), they are present as tempters for whose attractive offer one has to pay the price of resignation. These priests represent a fixed order which they consider infinitely valid; they are not tragic figures suffering from the situation. They have little in common with the priests of Graham Greene or with the main figure of Georges Bernanos' *Journal of a Country Priest* (1936). What is of concern

here is Christianity as a cultural system which Camus and
Malraux object to, and which they reject as a workable value
system.

Christian teachings suggest a belief in life after death. It
promises the possibility of grace on which grounds man can
expect salvation so that life and suffering can have meaning
for him. Camus and Malraux, in their earlier work, protest
against this hope of salvation and use the term "absurd." This
word, beginning with *Man's Fate*, is no longer used by Malraux
in this specific sense; for Camus the use ended prior to *The
Plague*; and in Kafka it is apparently absent. The word *absurd*,
then, seems to be directed against any form of transcendent
hope, every general chance for orientation.

If one reads Kafka's work as an inverted Christian theology,[13] it is made more dependent upon Western faith than it
really is. It can be suggested of the K.'s that they are on their
way to God or in search of the meaning of life, so long as it is
realized that the novels themselves never speak of it. If, however, Christian implication is denied, one ignores the cultural
system of the West of which Kafka was a part. The deductions
very much rest with the esthetic experience of the reader, and if
he is willing to grant "absurd" and "Christian" each a share of
the concept "modern," he cannot fail to see a relationship.
Every frame of reference, whether Christian or other, imposed
upon the fictional labyrinth of Kafka, nevertheless becomes a
blinder. The result becomes one of loss, of disorientation, and
leads to a feeling of absurdity. This sense of aloneness, pro-
duced by the interrelationship of preconception and actual experience, is also analyzed by Camus and Malraux. In their work
it produces strangers who do not know or who do not accept
the world inside the standard frame of reference.

The absence of generally recognized attitudes which mark
the route of one's identification with the world is not peculiar
to writers of absurdity. It is only typical of Camus and Malraux
that they recognize the situation as absurd and classify it as
such. They do not institute a new dogma or carry a message to
the reader. Like Malraux' Alvéar, the old art lover of *Man's
Hope*, they try to describe the world in spite of itself, knowing
that "neither philosopher nor novelist has any message. People

who deal in life are unavailing in the face of death. Wisdom is more vulnerable than beauty; because wisdom's an impure art."[14] Works which fall within the pale of conventional systems cannot survive solely by virtue of their wise moral and Christian message. They need to concentrate on man's consciousness in unfamiliar surroundings while he is caught between "n'est pas encore" and "ne peut pas être," to borrow from Paul Valéry.[15] When one takes novels like Melville's *Moby-Dick* (1851) or Dostoevsky's *The Possessed*, one realizes that their permanence is guaranteed by a lack of predetermined order within the internal narrative. In the case of Melville— disregarding the whaling history chapters—it is obvious that Father Mapple's sermon and Ishmael's contemplation in the graveyard are a dangling prologue to the narrative proper. It is a piece of religious commentary which introduces a story that is not yet ready to develop dramatically.[16] Furthermore, the description of the fate of Jonah imposes a conventional system which, by having been given undue importance, distracts from the tragedy about to follow. There is an incongruity between Jonah's role and the one of Ahab and his men in the tragic narrative. The lesson to be learned from Jonah's punishment is not conveyed through the novel, but is as "truth" limited to Melville's personal conviction. It is only after one ignores the requested attitude that the horror of Ahab's tragic fate can be experienced. The captain's "strangeness" can be known only if one disregards the common Christian norms— which is not to say that Ahab is not a religious figure. He is, in so far that other worlds can manifest themselves in him.

In spite of the fact that Dostoevsky gave his later novels a Christian message, his work still survives as a religious experience which is not determined by this message. His novels presuppose a society cast adrift under the leadership of a Church hierarchy and a group of intellectuals estranged from the people. Dostoevsky preached a Russian Christendom, and his great novels were meant to carry the message. Fortunately, his characters belong to their fictional world because they are made to live their religious experience. They are part of Dostoevsky's isolation, and they live his estrangement: Ivan is given Alyosha for salvation, Stavrogin has Shatov, and Rogozhin and

Ippolyt can turn to Myshkin. Because Dostoevsky made his characters the spokesmen of his religious doubt, his convictions and denials are communicable through them. His contemplations do not stand as a private truth aside the narrative proper. Myshkin is not the symbol of Christ because he voices the author's opinion that the suffering to which men subject each other has nothing to do with religion. He can symbolize Christ because he gladly shares the suffering of others. Stavrogin is not the symbol of evil because he preaches the denial of all values. He is the destroyer whose motivations Dostoevsky never explicitly states but allows the reader to deduce from the reactions of all "possessed" characters. Stavrogin and Myshkin are ideally portrayed: they draw the reader along the path of their search for an Absolute—be it good or evil—and when they finally recognize the futility of their quest, they have evoked the sense of estrangement which later novelists have praised. Camus, Malraux, and Kafka learned well, and in order to understand what "religious" has meant to them, the reader has to depend upon his esthetic experience when confronted with their fictional world.

Tarrou in *The Plague* wonders how one can become a saint without God. He is a disbeliever who tries his utmost to banish suffering, to understand everyone, and not to hurt his fellow man. Caligula, in the play which carries his name, knows a similar desire for unity, but for him it works in an opposite direction. Tarrou tries to practice a relativism; Caligula is an absolutist who subjugates all to his will and who, in refusing to understand, creates havoc at random. He looks for something that is not of this world: the moon, immortality, or whatever else it may be. So absolute is his desire that he has made relative everything around him—just as Tarrou has learned of this relativity which leaves him nothing but a kind of absolute sainthood where the ties with the world can be severed because they will be clearly defined. Both Caligula and Tarrou are religious figures, as well as eccentric and branded: the one because of his autonomous, cruel madness, the other because of his merciful sainthood at his own risk.

It is said about Tchen in *Man's Fate* that "There was something mad about this silent comrade meditating upon his familiar visions of horror, but also something sacred—as there always is about the presence of the inhuman."[17] Tchen cannot do anything else but murder. He has become the victim of the forces against which the figures in Malraux' work have to prove their condition of being man. Death, the mightiest opponent man meets in his life, has already taken possession of Tchen within his lifetime. Like Stavrogin, Dostoevsky's presentation in *The Possessed* of death-in-life, he is singled out to repel people because he fascinates them. Malraux and Dostoevsky use religious terminology when they write about human solidarity. To maintain their oneness, be it in Christian harmony with God or in atheistic union with mankind, men must share in the battle against the power of Death. Those who drift away from unity eventually die in the agony of aloneness. Man lives between these two extremes, these two poles which Camus defined as the solitary and the solidary state.

Tarrou's father was a judge. His son has realized that he attended the executions of those he had condemned to die. Ever since he has felt plagued by the nauseating memory, and he tries to redeem his father's guilt with acts of understanding and good deeds. Alyosha Karamazov does penance for his family in a similar manner. Caligula begins to indulge in his vicious whims after the death of his beloved sister: he subjects a world hostile to him, to his absolute will. Tchen becomes inhuman after his assassination of an enemy. All these characters act and react because of a father figure who is destructive, false, or absent. So it is with Kafka. His writing is defined by the ambivalent relation of K. to his father. Without conscious awareness, he feels a compulsion for self-punishment without ever being able to pay the moral debt. In all these cases man risks estrangement from himself and his world. He has been led to the border of no-man's-land where lurk lack of salvation and the imminence of death. An ambiguous father figure or paternal substitute is usually, within our religious cultural system, associated with annihilation. In "The Judgment" (1913) Kafka tells of a man who was sentenced to death by his father. Beckett's Estragon and Vladimir waste their lives in nothingness waiting for Godot. The narrator of *The Fall* calls mankind to a brotherhood of perpetual denial. Ahab's crew is destroyed in vengeance. Malraux' revolutionaries are eliminated by the system in which they sought refuge. In all these narratives, which employ religious types and Christian images, there is a given fictional reality with which the characters can identify and in which they can operate. It is *their* reality from which they become estranged. Tchen can still function within the Communist party. Caligula can for some time combine his caprices and his imperial functions. Tarrou, at odds with himself, is still with the vanguard in the battle against the plague. The solidarity they find is real, if short-lived. Katow, for example, has but the brief moment in which he gives away his poison before being burned alive. In these narratives something "strange" happens, which is unusual enough to bring the incident and the characters involved to the fore, yet not so different that they are transported beyond the fictional reality with which they and the reader have identified. One can only be estranged from the known and the identifiable. It is, to borrow one of Camus' examples of the absurd, a matter of looking at one's mirror image, not finding the expected, and thus discovering who one really is. In other words, the unfamiliar and the known oppose each other, and from this tension is born an insight, a transcending and visionary reality which can be termed "a kind of mystical sensation . . . a *Vie extérieure* of profound intensity."[18]

To say that the awareness of this visionary experience is limited to our century would be incorrect. The necessity to impart this quality to a work of art had already been perceived by Charles Baudelaire. In his *Salon de 1846* he said that Romanticism, among many things, is an "aspiration towards the infinite, expressed by every means available to the arts."[19] In the succeeding years there has continued this uninterrupted realization that art, as aspiration toward the infinite, possesses a "quasi-theological" quality: "the end of art as such is not to know, but to produce or *create* . . . in the way of the spirit and of liberty."[20] What is meant here with the word "create" is the mental act of conjuring up a vision of a transcendent reality. In a superb study on the nature of literary interpretation Murray Krieger has spoken of this vision as it has developed in the past one hundred years. Man acts in the tragedy of life and becomes confronted with the amorality of the universe. He discovers that his moral assumptions are inadequate to cope with his experience. Unable to synthesize the contradiction, he has a "tragic vision" of life's absurdity. In literature which deals with the "normal" man converted to the "exceptional" man, there must be, Krieger further maintains, for the reader a balance of necessities between the tragic and the Absolute. These opposites, poised against each other, are "to create the unresolvable tension that must now replace tragedy's more sublime catharsis as the principle of aesthetic control." The "vision" of the fictional character, the "visionary," must be "a vision of extreme cases, a distillate of the rebellion, the godlessness which, once introduced by crisis, purifies itself by rejecting all palliatives. And the tragic visionary, by the stark austerity of his ontological position and of his dramatic position in the fable, is the extremist who—despite his rich intermingling with the stuff of experience—finds himself transformed from character to parable."[21] This transformation "to parable" suggests the moral Absolute, and as such it partakes of the "religious."[22] As a type of insight on the part of the "tragic visionary," it can lead to salvation in a solidarity with mankind as is the case with Dr. Rieux, Prince Myshkin, or Kassner of Malraux' *Days of Wrath* (1935). Even if the vision is denied, there is still the need to escape from aloneness. Clamence, Stavrogin, and Ahab deny transcendence, but in their search for a type of solidarity they seek companionship. The first group of fictional characters succeeds because they do not reject the human; the second group fails because they deny this bond.

The reader, caught in what Krieger termed the "unresolvable tension," may identify with the moment of confrontation in which the individual risks estrangement. Passively, he can be aware of loss and, with the patricians, feel threatened by Caligula (in Camus' play of the same name, 1944) or, with Ahab's crew, be sailed to destruction. Actively, the reader can enter the tension with the "strange" character and become the outsider rather than the norm. Once "outside" he is allowed a glimpse of the transcendent or of what Rudolph Otto has called

"Das Ganz Andere," the Wholly Other, where he can partake
of a numinous experience.[23]

The stranger can be considered a figure in whom the otherness takes form because he is other than the people around him.
This is clearly the case with Meursault and Joseph K., whom
the reader, in awe, follows to their judgment after alienation
from their environment. In these two instances the reader can
only join K. and Meursault. However, in novels like *The Plague*,
The Royal Way, or *The Idiot* (1868), where the characters
struggle to readjust to a changed environment, the reader is
offered a clearly marked choice. Rieux is, within the world of
the novel, the "ideal" man who has come to help "ordinary"
people. His presence suggests hope to the plague-stricken and
redemption in a brotherhood of healing. He is the other in that
he knows that the plague bacilli never die or disappear for good.
The reader, like Rieux' friends, can accept him or reject his
vision that in man there is more to admire than to despise.
Malraux presents the reader with Perken who is other, not
only because he has rejected Western society, but also because
he knows that man is a prisoner of destiny. At the conclusion
of the novel, his younger companion wants to embrace him as
he is dying, but Perken gazes at him as if he is a stranger, "an
intruder from another world."[24] One can resolve the tension
and accept Perken's newly found realm where one escapes one's
destiny or enjoy Claude's brief, "religious" experience of
desperate fraternity. Prince Myshkin is other because he is not
part of the sensual world of "normal" people. The "sane" ob-
serve that he is an "idiot." His exceptional position is laden
with ambivalences. The fictional characters which surround him
are both fascinated and repelled by the Prince, while the reader,
in turn, is fascinated and repelled by them. The nature of this
tension developed within the fictional world, the reader can
recognize. It is more difficult, however, to determine the nature
of the ambivalence when the other stands alone in the center
of the novel, unaccompanied and absurd in his solitary state.
Rieux, Perken, and Myshkin are part of the other which surround them; Meursault and Joseph K. lack this identity in their
fictional world, and it is up to the reader to move into the
emptiness. However, the invitation to the reader also carries

an ambivalent effect. Meursault and Joseph K. are fascinating because they lead man to a point of contact with aloneness, but they also make him recoil because of the intimation of death inherent in aloneness. Both strangers are condemned to die and in this they differ from Myshkin who becomes deranged, from Perken who wills his fate, and from Rieux who remains to admire the living and the dead.

If one considers the principle of otherness as a particular category within the esthetic experience and calls it "religious," one can call the strangers already discussed "religious" figures. Yet, by employing such a limitation one can tamper with the artistic moment the author presented. The strangers *are* different from their environment, the reader's attitude *is* one of ambivalence and not of affirmation, but their otherness cannot be defined without the fictional world in which they live. The elements which set the stranger apart can be justly analyzed, but those aspects which testify to their otherness are then easily ignored. There is the danger that emphasis on the "religious" characteristics of the stranger lifts him prematurely from the reader's esthetic experience where, in a sense, he was created.

The author has thrown out a challenge to which the reader will insist on finding an answer. The most obvious way of creating a frame of reference is to discover the author's motivation for writing what he wrote. If, for example, one wants to know why Dostoevsky created *The Possessed*, it is helpful to know that he had a horror of political crimes and wanted to warn his contemporaries of the dangers of nihilism. But, actually, the motivation is secondary. What is needed is an analysis of the thought expressed and the language used. Kirillov's expression of his need to become a man-god is haltingly put forth, in the appropriate manner of a man who seldom speaks and mostly reflects on his fate. His aim is clearly outlined and his disconnected expressions suggest a thinker out of touch with the world.

In the twentieth century Kirillov's literary descendants no longer try to be explicit when they propose and dispose. If one considers the isolation of Tchen, the mutilation of Grabot, the destruction of the Renegade (from Camus' short story of the same title [1957]), or, for that matter, the enigmatic presence of the stranger, their language is reduced to guttural non-sense syllables or to vaguely expressed meaning. There are suggestions of the unknown, the dissimilar, the mysterious, the alien, which indicate that man is transcending himself and his world —that is, that he experiences a reality which is beyond his observation and his rational awareness. They are words which already were part of the Romantic cult. As Mario Praz has it: "Bacon had already expressed the idea (that Poe never tired of quoting and Baudelaire repeated after him) that 'there is no excellent beauty that hath not some strangeness in the proportion.' "[25] The strangeness meant here is the "spooky," the bizarre, the fatal, the secret of the night, the macabre, and sinful attraction, which are all related to sexuality.[26] The black magic of love brings man in contact with an elusive reality which is prematurely rationalized in an industrializing world. Surrealism also has a preference for what is different from the ordinary. The Surrealistic artist resembles his Romantic predecessor, but he lives under still greater pressure in a state of *inquiétude* brought on by threats of cosmic warfare. Surrealism is more aggressive, more criminal, and more politically minded than Romanticism. The strangeness is related to the mysterious, the infamous, the absurd, and it challenges complacency with interpretations which can also be found in Romanticism but which in Surrealism are often exploited for their own sake. The revolt in Surrealism is more pronounced than in Romanticism. "Revolution . . . Revolution . . . Realism is the pruning of trees, surrealism is the pruning of life," say the editors of *La Révolution Surréaliste*.[27] The artists of this movement believed in their own magical qualities and in the "miracle of art." "The work itself of the writer, and particularly of the poet, was seen more and more to be a magical incantation, an evocative magic or witchcraft whose creation and whose effect were both miraculous. The artistic work might be compared to the 'host' of sacramental Christianity which contains the 'real presence.' "[28] The surrealist is the manager of otherness. In this lie the power and the weakness of this movement and of related artistic experimentations. Their efforts, which cleared the literary ground for the future developments of a Malraux and a Camus, were vulnerable to the inherent danger of confusing a manifesto with an artistic creation, as André Breton's *Nadja* (1928) bears out.

Camus has not wanted to develop in Caligula a figure in whom a mysterious otherness is manifested. He has created a Caligula in whom this takes place after all. First there is Caligula, only then the otherness of his appearance. This cause and effect should not be reversed. No one begins with the world on the other side of this existence. When Sartre created Orestes in *The Flies*, he had his hero discover that "la vie humaine commence de l'autre côté du désespoir" (Act III). This far side of despair where human life begins has had its source in *this* life, and the artist, describing the events, should arrive at the strange. The otherness can be theistically interpreted as a revelation in which man becomes invisible, in which the human disappears. It is an awareness where he transcends himself and comes in contact with a "religious" aspect of the esthetic experience. If, like Dante, the artist begins his artistic moment on the other side, leaving the reader to fill in the knowledge of *this* world, one is led to a personal confrontation with the artist. The experience is predetermined as in the world of Kafka with its conflict between the individual and authority, and the world of Dostoevsky with its clash of good and evil in the heart of man. It is also possible for the artist to create the existence of the known world and leave the reader to a realization of otherness. In this case one confronts the impersonal work of art, and the reader is left a multiple choice of private interpretation. The disembodied presence of "No. 1" in Arthur Koestler's *Darkness at Noon* (1940), the absence of Godot, and the presumed presence of Kurtz in Joseph Conrad's *Heart of Darkness* (1902) are moments of suspension and of silence within the esthetic experience. They are instants where the artist has left a blank for a personal vision on the part of the reader. With the imprisoned Rubashov, with Estragon and Vladimir, with Marlow the waiting and the search become a fact. With them one fluctuates between the general and the personal, the lack of certainty and the private vision.

This vacillating movement is an estrangement which takes

shape in the figure of the stranger. The main characteristic of this fictional type is, of course, that one cannot recognize him, but one has to define his appeal so that one can associate with him. In identifying with the stranger's anonymity and using him as a mirror of one's self, one begins to move back and forth to get the image in satisfactory perspective. The point of rest becomes relocated and the lost equilibrium of the displaced world has to be restabilized. Thus, the tension of the work of literary art has its source in the stranger, whether he is present, absent, or a disembodied reality. Camus experimented with all three categories: there is Meursault, there is the departed God in *The Plague*, and there is Clamence in *The Fall*. Without any one of these realities no ambivalence would exist in the given world of the fiction.

In partial summary it can be said that estrangement leads to a labile equilibrium within the confrontation of self and other, which, in turn, can lead to a transcending or "religious" aware-ness. Some critics have called the work of Kafka religious either because they expect the presence of a godhead in the hidden courtroom or in the Castle, or because they see these places as symbols of God's inaccessibility.[29] It is, however, not necessary to speculate because gods *are* present in Kafka's fictional world. They are described, but one cannot really say that they exist or that they do not exist. Their existence is determined solely by the reality the fictional characters are willing to ascribe to them. In *The Trial* Titorelli is painting a judge in a chair, a judge who, at times, resembles a goddess (Ch. VII). In *Amerika* (1927) there are trumpet blowers, in front of the Nature theater of Oklahoma, dressed as angels (Ch. VIII). In *The Castle* K. dreams that he defeats a secretary who resembles a Grecian god (Ch. XVIII). The gods of Kafka become a reality within the word-picture only and, within this created image which one can "see," the instability of the situation is intensified. They all appear at the end of the novel where their apparition is a question rather than an answer. Will Rossmann's problems be solved in a theater almost as large as the world? Will K. be able to mollify the secretary? Will the judges eventually de-stroy Joseph K.? These divinities are fortuitous, and they only serve to illustrate the situation, which is of endless perspective. When Joseph K. asks Titorello to explain the painting, the latter continues his work to clarify the picture. With every stroke of the crayon a new image is created behind the already existing image until suddenly a goddess appears, and then another one, and another one. In Kafka's multidimensional world divinities *can* exist, and in so doing they create a limit. The character can realize that they are a fake because they are only a painting. Yet, his certainty is canceled out because he does not know if the goddess is meant to hide something. The intent of the judges is still not revealed. The gods of Kafka reflect the estrangement of the main characters of his novels. They find themselves in a situation beyond their comprehension but which they, at all cost, have to master. Within the esthetic experience of the reader, gods are necessary but outside this confrontation they fade within the image. They are not like Dostoevsky's spiders and devils who can exist in other frameworks. The "religious" awareness is nullified in Kafka's work. The goddess in Titorello's chair must return to non-being.

The god whom Beckett calls Godot differs from her in that he is invisible. The situation with which the spectator of *Waiting for Godot* is confronted shows that he has not (yet) arrived. The (non-)existence of Godot is only important in so far as it gives meaning to the existence of Estragon and Vladimir. Waiting for Godot, they kill time, trying to guess a reason for being instead of accepting life. Here, too, within the esthetic experience, there is a true relation between estrangement and religion —although the path leads from religion to estrangement. In this case there is a reversal of the experiences so far discussed. In Kafka's world the alienation suddenly becomes acute, and a god appears. In Beckett's play his absence is so conspicuous that the world of the characters loses all stability. Estragon and Vladimir begin to act like clowns pretending that they exist. Without Godot their individual characteristics have become irrelevant. This slowly developing lack of identity is transmitted to the world of the spectator and with those on stage one drifts away to a point of futility and nothingness.

With Godot the strangers have in common that they function as a center of estrangement. Something, therefore, is wrong with their name or they lack that type of identification with which man can define himself. Whereas, for example, Stephen Dedalus in Joyce's portrait of his youth finds release from estrangement when he becomes conscious of the prophetic quality of his name, the stranger is not so lucky, and his name is merely a label by which others identify him. Meursault is a dead mother's son, a girl's lover, and a pimp's friend. He remains anonymous until he becomes a murderer—at which point he is transformed into an identifiable reality. With the people in the courtroom he is able to say: I, Meursault, the murderer. Only on the verge of death does he realize a "nameful" relationship with the universe. In *The Fall* this anonymity is less clear. The strangeness is obviously a masquerade and a deliberate deception. Jean-Baptiste has a name when he enters, but he admits later that it is a pseudonym. His strangeness is equivocal; his anonymity is "played." In *The Possessed* the stranger has a name. Namelessness does not seem to be the case, but it soon becomes clear that Stavrogin is a façade behind which people *secretly* relate to him. His indifference mirrors their anguish. He is the "undercover" stranger as opposed to Stephen Dedalus who only seemingly is an outsider. The insiders who help him reconcile the conflicting aspects of the self he welcomes. Apparently, society does not always turn the protagonist into an outcast. Meursault, Garine, and K. were set adrift by the judgment of the world. Another category are those who recognize this danger, wish to avoid destruction at the hand of others, and condemn themselves.

This theme of self-condemnation can be traced back to Dostoevsky's underground narrator who is charged with hatred for himself and the world at large. The question is, how did this hatred originate? Apparently, it has had its source in frustrated aspiration; that is, faith has been placed in a false promise from the outside. For Dostoevsky's anti-hero it has been, as it was for Cain, a promise of justice. Once they discovered the deception, they sought refuge in an autonomous state. God is unjust; man must take his place. Pride of intellect has always been a temptation, but in fierce defiance it becomes amplified; and as it swells, the consciousness of existence becomes solitary and contemptuous. In solitude man discovers that the promise is false, but, unable to convey this experience, he remains alone and so descends into a hell of private disappointment. The underground man has hoped to find communion in solidarity and share his sorrow of frustration. But his was an empty hope since he gambled with nothing at stake. He loudly proclaimed that he did not wish to change his being and that he was self-sufficient. His pride could survive only with the help of a lie, and the lie was sustained with the desire for self-preservation. Dostoevsky's mouse-like hero differs radically from Malraux' fighters who are willing to seek solidarity in communal action against opposing forces, from Camus' Dr. Rieux who opposed fate in his defiance of death, and from the Joseph K.'s who are at the mercy of something they cannot define. Dostoevsky's underground man has defined this something and he has passed on this awareness to his literary descendants. Dostoevsky recreated him in the character of Stavrogin, Camus imitated him with the portrayal of Clamence, and lastly, although he is not a Dostoevsky-inspired hero,[30] Herman Melville developed Ahab, an American equivalent of the self-castigators. These heroes have realized the false promise of justice; they have ceased to yearn for innocence and participation in a brotherhood of suffering. They think solidarity a sham because in solidarity there is the risk of expulsion and judgment, and, since at all costs a second breach of promise must be avoided, they create a world of their own making. To the outside it appears that their self-sufficiency is a divine inheritance, and so the excluded turn toward them for guidance. They inspire faith and those who are attracted think they need only to discover their secret to enjoy the same brilliant future of gratified yearning. "The denial of God does not eliminate transcendence; it deflects this aspiration from the 'beyond' to the 'here.' The imitation of Christ becomes the imitation of one's neighbor."[31]

As Camus implied, man needs to turn to someone other to relieve the tension of estrangement. Clamence, Stavrogin, and Ahab realize that man looks in vain, and they move in as divine substitute to fill the void. To understand them the reader must look at them as models and consider their relation with their followers, the possessed, who live by the ideas of their idols.

They regard them with both admiration and hatred, a mixture which characterizes most leader-disciple relationships. The world of the possessed is a parody of the Christian one. The sincere mediation of Christ and His prophets is replaced by the selfish interference of advocates of anguish and hate. The listeners in *The Fall*, the nihilists in *The Possessed*, and Ahab's crew in *Moby-Dick* offer to their leader everything that is most precious to them: their hope in redemption. Unfortunately, their transcendency, as Camus saw it in *The Fall*, is horizontal. There is no aspiration to ascend. It is man-directed in a world where God is either dead or unapproachable.

False prophets promise salvation in a brotherhood of complicity, and they proclaim the way; they claim to provide the chart to the labyrinth of estrangement and suggest ways to alleviate the guilt man feels in having contributed to mankind's separation from innocence. They are treacherous because they herald paradise while leading their people into their private hell where they are to perish in aloneness. They are the false gods with a human face who know that absolute freedom is unbearable. They capitalize on the anguish of Fatherless men and become, in the manner of Stavrogin, the flag on which mankind can fix his eyes. They realize that man needs identification with otherness, and so they choose to become the godheads for those who cannot give up their longing for eternity. Clamence, Stavrogin, and Ahab are like the gods of Kafka's fictional world in that they provide a perceptional limit for the characters who surround them. They can be recognized as a fake, but if those seeking protective bounds were to do so, the offered security would be destroyed. The hope is that they know the gate to salvation, but their falsely prophetic intent is seldom revealed. These emissaries of the Void reflect the estrangement of the novels' characters, but unlike Kafka's gods they do not fade for the reader outside his esthetic experience. The terrible vision of the parody of religious experience lingers on.

The Fall, The Possessed, and *Moby-Dick* create a vision within the esthetic experience of the reader which is, in part, determined by the relationship of the content and form of these novels. To understand this relationship it is helpful to turn to

Nietzsche. In *The Birth of Tragedy* (1872) the German philosopher sees in tragedy the union of Apollonian and Dionysian motives or, in the terminology of Western religion, Christian and anti-Christian forces which resist and yet complement each other. Apollo is the god of light, the marvelous image that radiates the full delight, wisdom, and beauty of illusion; his counter-image Dionysus is the essence of rapture and physical intoxication. In Greek culture, as expressed in their tragedy, there is a perfect blending of these two opposing forces: "This enchantment is the prerequisite of all dramatic art. In this enchantment the Dionysian reveller sees himself as a satyr, *and as satyr he in turn beholds the god,* that is, in his transformation he sees a new vision outside him as the Apollonian consummation of his state. With this new vision the drama is complete."[32] If one denies the Dionysian, Nietzsche further comments, if one becomes a "Socratic" moralizer, one does not create tragedy but one destroys it. The conflict is removed and only the rigid boundary lines remain. If, on the other hand, there should be the Dionysian without the Apollonian, life would be infinitely chaotic and (self-)destructive. In effect, says Krieger discussing Nietzsche's essay: "It would be like tragedy without that moment in which the play comes round and the cosmos is saved and returned to us intact. It would be, in other words, the tragic vision wandering free of its capacious home in tragedy. . . . And the alienated members, now unchallenged, would be free to turn inward upon themselves to nourish their indignation in the dark underground."[33] This is precisely what happened in the nineteenth century when the Christian God of Light was eliminated from the thought of Western man. The "alienated members" turned inward and disappeared underground waiting for a substitute Creator of rigid boundary lines. It is the artist's awareness of this condition which tempts him to depict a Stavrogin and an Ahab, which, later, brings about a Clamence.

After the ancient Grecian culture had run its course, when Shakespearian and Racinian drama had come and gone, Western culture had passed its "tragic moment." It had to wait two hundred years to accommodate the ancient vision in a new genre. It remained for Dostoevsky and Melville to turn the novel to the uses of tragedy.[34] It was the subject matter, the trials of the hero, which had to be newly defined to make him representative of the age. To create the necessary support of a traditional sense of unity characteristic of tragedy Dostoevsky and Melville resorted to the dramatic or, in Northrop Frye's words, to the "high mimetic" mode in fiction.[35] The "new" hero struggled "not so much with a crisis as with a condition" and, worse, without a "clear and present opponent."[36] How then to adapt a classical form to contain the ill-defined involvement of a central action? The matters to be considered in such an adaptation would be dialogue (or monologue), limited point of view, and a verisimilitude of the unities of time and place.

To return to Nietzsche once more. In early Greek tragedy, it seems, the only reality on stage was the chorus, which created a vision out of itself and proclaimed it through dance, music, and words. "This chorus beholds in the vision its lord and master Dionysus, and it is thus for ever the *serving* chorus: it sees how he, the god, suffers and glorifies himself, and therefore does not itself act."[37] As Nietzsche saw it, so Dostoevsky and Melville might have perceived of this dramatic possibility. In *The Possessed* and *Moby-Dick* they reduced the characters who surround Stavrogin and Ahab to supporting players (including the narrator), who serve their godhead. Camus, who experimented with the same mode in *The Fall*, eliminated the chorus altogether by making its function part of the protagonist's role; he thereby restricted the dramatic point of view with the result that the work approximates, in this respect, ancient tragedy. Malraux, when speaking of this form, succinctly put it as follows: "The world of tragedy, is the ancient world still—man, the crowd, the elements, woman, destiny. It reduces itself to two characters, the hero and his sense of life."[38] In order not to distract from the hero and his sense of life, a narrator is employed to perform a threefold function. He is essential for the proper development of content in that he sketches in the background, provides continuity, and universalizes the dramatic experience. Further, he focuses attention on the action of the present moment by reducing past and off-stage action to a minimum. For the omniscient author there is the opportunity to refrain from intruding and, in so doing, from allowing the reader's imagination to lose itself in time. His dramatic method should convey "the psychological equivalent of the dramatic present"; and as Joseph Beach summarizes it: "The dramatic method is the method of direct presentation, and aims to give the reader the sense of being present, here and now, in the scene of the action. That is why those elements are undramatic which make us aware of an author explaining things."[39] The dramatic moment becomes a sequence of the "here and now" of each scene and as such one can speak of a unity of time, an uninterrupted chronological progression of events in time. This continuous present is well executed by Melville in *Moby-Dick*, and brought to perfection by Camus in *The Fall*. The dramatic method is successfully pursued when it enables the reader to merge the fictional time of the book with his own fictional present, and creates in him the illusion of being present, both in the sense of "now" and in the sense of watching an action on stage.

Because a stage effect is to be created, the reader should not be distracted by an ever-changing background or setting. The décor should be a part of a character's reaction at a given moment or it should contribute to the development of his emotional awareness. This aspect of the dramatic moment can be designated as the unity of place, that is, the setting should complement the action and be kept fairly constant according to the requirements of the "here."

The illusion of presentness also heavily depends upon the use of dialogue which produces an effect similar to that of the theater where one witnesses an action of which it is assumed that one is not a part. "Drama is a *mimesis* of dialogue or conversation," says Frye;[40] but, of course, if a novel were all dialogue, it would change genres and become a play. As Mendilow suggested, a solution to this difficulty would be indirect speech.[41] The compromise of direct and reported dialogue would not betray the fictional genre, while allowing the reader to identify the characters who are not, as in a play, physically present. In *The Fall* Camus solved this problem in an interesting manner. He wrote the *récit* as a monologue and reported only the narrator's side of any dialogue which occurred. By making the reader the "listener" to the endless flow of words and by inviting him to move in as the imaginary partner in the non-recorded side of the dialogue, he diminishes the separateness of character and reader in bringing the latter "on stage." The reader is invited to interpret, and, in doing so, he participates. He comes close to the action and is made to live it, rather than contemplate it. In other words, esthetic distance has been reduced to a minimum.

It is my contention that novels which employ the dramatic method are highly suited to the depiction of prophetic characters. These emissaries from Elsewhere require a limelight and a raised platform in order to be noticed. Since they give the illusion of divine self-sufficiency, they must represent an order —an order which an author can suggest by casting his subject matter into a mold of unity. This semblance of unity, however, serves an additional purpose. It creates a tension within the literary work of art: the moral and psychological chaos of the content belies the artistic presentation, which implies an ordered universe.

Camus in *The Fall*, Dostoevsky in *The Possessed*, and Melville in *Moby-Dick* suggest a five-act classical tragedy and present a world of tragic conflict under domination of false leaders. Jean-Baptiste Clamence, Nikolay Stavrogin, and Captain Ahab are depicted as heroes larger than life, who bring down their world when they fall from the high station they occupy. Their reign is established on the treacherous foundation of wrath upon the inexplicable forces which have broken down the wall of contentment with satisfactory reality. In other words, they have met with the "absurd."

To take revenge for what they consider a personal insult, they must gather an army for their destructive mission against the established order. They need converts for their zealous goal and they persuade the disenchanted, the noncommitted, and the unaware that their insight can guarantee a Utopia, any Utopia, to be defined after the revolutionary action has been completed. Sometimes these self-appointed rulers wonder why they were born to set a displaced order right, but, like Hamlet, they must reject everything which can create a human bond.

The authors suggest that life is only lived to the fullest in contention with opposing forces. But as spokesmen they leave little doubt that the secret for happiness in this contest lies in the recognition of each man's solidarity with mankind. The rejection of this factor becomes man's undoing. This flaw in his inflexible determination turns him into a false prophet and destroyer of the macrocosm he rules.

The reader, watching this enactment of monomania, and tempted by the presentness of the performers, moves into the empty spot which the author has provided, and so, within the esthetic experience, the reader vacillates between the poles of horrid fascination and mitigated repulsion. Yet, an acceptance of the vision as desirable would go against the author's intent. Since the works are meant as an analysis of their times, they should therefore be the mirror in which warning and reflection meet to trap the uneasy Christian conscience of the reader.

3

Camus' The Fall

WHEN ALBERT CAMUS' *récit The Fall* WAS PUB-
lished in 1956, it met with a critical opinion that stressed the
work's ambiguities. Most reviewers reacted favorably, but,
unsure of Camus' purpose, they tended to regard it as inferior
to *The Plague*. Many subsequent critics have agreed that the
work lends itself to various interpretations: "Difficult to interpret with certainty," as John Cruickshank wrote,[1] or, in Germaine Brée's words, a work only to be understood "as a
parable,"[2] an opinion supported by Carl Viggiani's discussion
of the *récit*.[3] Jean-Paul Sartre's commentary of the same year
tends to confirm the Anglo-American observation.[4] The remarks of these critics have remained valid, and much of the
interpretive criticism which followed is in agreement with them.
It appears that only those commentators who have studied the
form of *The Fall*, and those who have looked for literary ante-
cedents, can let the issue rest.

It is difficult to find a satisfactory relationship between the
parts of *The Fall* because of an incongruity between content and
form. The narrator's account of his past is not necessarily true
(he admits to lying), and his commentary on the present is
biased, while the simple form in which the false avowal is arranged gives a wrong impression of order.

The narration consists of six confessions. The first one explains the presence of the speaker in the particular setting, and his role in life; the next five relate the past experiences of the protagonist to his present function in life. If this first part is called a Prologue, in which the scene is set and the characters are introduced, the remaining parts may well suggest the five-act classical tragedy with a unity of time and place maintained.[5] The unity of time is suggested by the nocturnal or sunless hours in which the confessions are made, a time of darkness without end, a perpetual void. The unity of place is obviously the bourgeois hell of dis-eased complacency within the concentric circles of the Amsterdam canals that connect with a dead sea.

If, however, the time elapsed in the telling of the confession is considered, the five nights might make up the five acts. Carl Viggiani, taking the woman's suicide on the bridge as the crucial point in the narration, observes that this "is the climax in the symmetrically structured narrative, occurring at the end of the third day (there are five) of the confession and at the conclusion of the third chapter (there are six),"[6] which would coincide with the classical concept of epitasis, or turning point, in the third act. Maurice Blanchot[7] is also interested in *The Fall* as a close relative of classical tragedy and, after having referred to the *récit* as a "dialogue solitare" and its narrator's relation to Oedipus (both speak to silent skies and retired gods), he goes on to list its classical characteristics. They are "l'impersonalité des traits," generality of character, details which do not convey something unique, and, lastly, excluding the last scene of remorse (which might have been borrowed from Stendhal), "cette confession dédaigneuse qui ne confesse rien où l'on puisse reconnaître quelque expérience vécue" (this disdainful confession which confesses nothing in which one can recognize some realistic experience). Brée, undoubtedly aware of all these elements, summed up these observations by referring to Camus' fictional *oeuvre* as worlds "which recall the closed self-contained universe of classical tragedy."[8]

It is plausible that these critical observations were suggested by a 1960 interview which Camus gave to the literary magazine *Venture*. The original French version has been reprinted in Paul Ginestier's study of Camus. In this discussion Camus had the

following to say about *The Fall:* "I have used here a technique
of the theatre (the dramatic monologue and the implicit dialogue) to describe a tragic comedian. I have adapted the form
to suit the subject. That is all."[9]

Two other dimensions are suggested by this statement. The
protagonist of the "play" is a "tragic comedian" who uses a
"dramatic monologue" while being the sole performer ("implicit dialogue") on the stage. This tragic comedian plays for an
audience guilty of murder and unconcern for mankind. In the
performance he attempts to catch its conscience and bring about
a catharsis; hence, Camus' choice to cast the *récit* into the
classical dramatic form. The play takes place within the play
mankind performs, and the dramatic monologue of the speaker
is a reflection of the modern communiqué, which has replaced
the exchange of ideas essential for a harmonious existence. The
wit of the comedian is very entertaining and aims for the stray-
ing bourgeois, "le bourgeois qui s'égare"—the players on the
stage of life-intelligent. These players, in their fascination, are
drawn into the game of complicity in guilt to be destroyed:
"The most sensitive among them tried to understand me, and
that effort led them to melancholy surrenders" (61).[10] The
comedian mirrors the miserable condition of mankind which
itself has lost human dignity; and since in the modern world
any value is as good as the next, the clownish performer
proffers his friendly solution once his audience is trapped: to
become One in a democracy of guilt to replace all the defunct
systems man has set up since the day his Unity in God was
destroyed in Eden. Man has drifted away in exile on separate
islands, without communion and without communication, toward a negative landscape where everything is "horizontal" and
man is alone with his other self. Our saving comedian speaks to
gather the other selves into his haven of one-mindedness. The
new Unifier on stage is a character of insidious intent who,
after he has brought about a conversion, admits that he spoke
not necessarily of truth but only tried to "construct a portrait
which is the image of all and no one. A mask, in short, rather
like those carnival masks which are both lifelife and stylized,
so that they make people say: 'Why, surely I've met him!' "
(139).

He is alone, above the crowd,[11] with no one to share the limelight, and all eyes are directed at him. He has placed himself in this advantageous position to be well seen and well heard as a speaker who is announcing a better tomorrow. The mask he wears hides the microcosm within, the *paysage démoralisé*, the desert hidden behind the painted portrait of the Promised Land that tempts the converts-to-be.

The use of the implicit dialogue helps to create the discomfort essential for the action of conversion, the recognition of guilt which may lead to repentance and next to the admission to the brotherhood of betrayal. In this implicit dialogue only the narrator's part in the conversation with an interchangeable other is related, and the audience is left to wonder how well the unheard side is acknowledged or interpreted by the speaker. The monologue masquerading as dialogue (a well-coined critics' phrase) goes on and on until everyone present is convinced that *he* is the other. Then the comedian's obligation to mankind is fulfilled: Man, having become aware of his vile state, can now "justly" betray and pronounce judgment on his fellow men.

The monologue purports to be a confession of the narrator's sins of omission and acts of treason by having done, as T. S. Eliot writes in *Murder in the Cathedral*, the "right deed for the wrong reason" (Thomas Becket's last speech of Part I). The confessional account follows no chronological order—the incidents related are arranged in increasing order of the seriousness involved in the sin committed. The manner in which the confessions are made—slanted, to stress the despicable in the narrator's life and to place the commendable in a ridiculous light—brings to the fore the speaker's purpose: to lead mankind to a slavery that will reunite man. As Marcel Arland has put it: "Tous les hommes sont nés pour la servitude; dans la fraternité du mal, Clamence sera leur conscience, leur voix et leur maître."[12] (All men are born for servitude; in the brotherhood of evil, Clamence will be their conscience, their voice and their master.)

Jean-Baptiste Clamence, the narrator of *The Fall*, conducts court in a bar in Amsterdam and invites all those interested in "la servitude" to join him. His name is a marvelous pun on John

the Baptist who was a *vox clamans in deserto*, a voice crying
out in the desert, "Repent ye: for the kingdom of heaven is at
hand." "And the same John had his raiment of camel's hair";
Jean-Baptiste does too. Only his coat, as he quips, was prob-
ably woven from the hair of a camel with mange. John the
Baptist prepares a way for a savior who will bring clemency (a
possibility for the pun in the name Clamence); Jean-Baptiste
prepares a way for the perpetuation of the void. John the Baptist
preaches outside Jerusalem and gathers a following; Jean-
Baptiste advocates judgment far away from Paris—the place
where he was happy once—to those who came out of mytho-
mania and ignorance. To his following Jean-Baptiste proclaims
himself to be the beginning and the end of the recognition of
man's complicity.

When the *récit* opens, we are at the first night of confession.
Clamence has met a compatriot, apparently a likely victim, to
whom he tells the story of his adult life. Once, as the story goes,
he had been a brilliant Parisian lawyer. The years were a joy of
self-satisfaction, but it was not to last. One autumn evening he
is returning home and, while crossing the Pont Royal, he notices
a woman standing at the railing. He admires her lovely neck
but does not stop. Continuing along, he suddenly hears the
splash of a body hitting the water, followed by screams
diminishing in the distance. Clamence pauses to listen. He
trembles. Cowardice takes hold of him. Yet, recollecting the
occurrence later, in his confessional monologue, he claims a
momentary confusion, one which has found its origin in the
belief that the woman must almost at once have drowned. He
goes away into the night, having ignored the attempted suicide
and insisting to do so thereafter by not reading the newspapers
the following days. Clamence prefers to forget that he has let
Innocence die.

Some years pass and again on his way home one evening,
this time as he crosses the Pont des Arts, his peace of mind is
threatened. For a moment Clamence lingers to enjoy an island
in the Seine when loud laughter bursts out behind him. He tries
to find the source, but the laughter recedes and he sees no one.
That night there is laughter under his bedroom window. When
he looks out, there are only a few young men in the street say-

ing good night to each other. From that moment on Clamence begins to look at himself in relation to the world around him. With the implied derision the "stage sets" have collapsed and Clamence becomes confronted with the "absurd" as Camus described it in *The Myth of Sisyphus* (1942). Clamence's consciousness is awakened with the realization that the evening "when the music stopped, the lights went out" (30). He is now made to recognize the discrepancy between the way the world is and the way he perceives it to be.

He realizes that to condescend to treat hopeless cases is nothing but self-exultation which affords the chance to rise above colleagues and society. Returning to his consciousness are also the incidents in his life which showed up his pettiness and cowardice. There was the time he hesitated to hit back an attacker until the moment had passed; and the time he asked that a beggar be removed from his presence for disturbing the joy of a good lunch; and the time in a concentration camp in Tripolis when he drank the water of a dying man, while convincing himself that his life was of more use to his fellow-prisoners than the one of the man about to die.

Clamence realizes that he lives, in what he calls, a "malconfort" (a "little-ease"). It is a type of medieval cell not high enough to stand up in yet not wide enough to allow lying down. A man living within these ingenious dimensions has to live "on the diagonal" (109)—much like the Jonah of Father Mapple's sermon in *Moby-Dick*, who notices the "obliquity" of the cabin in the ship of his escape. Within these fixed restrictions of their surroundings these two are constantly reminded of their guilt through physical unease. Clamence now beings to seek for escape from judgment and hopes for a love to set him free; unfortunately, his self-love keeps him imprisoned. "It was not love or generosity that awakened me when I was in danger of being forsaken, but merely the desire to be loved and to receive what in my opinion was due me. The moment I was loved and my partner again forgotten, I shone, I was at the top of my form, I became likable" (66–67). Clamence considers suicide but he resists, thinking his friends will find it vulgar and idiotic. In a last attempt to shake off his self-accusation Clamence plunges into debauchery, liberating because it creates no obligation, to find that it is but a long sleep. And so, at last, he leaves Paris for Amsterdam: the Gabriel of lucidity has shown Clamence the way out of his state of blessed content.

To Camus this Northern City is a kind of hell for the bourgeois, a nice place to practice a calling as "'juge-pénitent." In this profession a confessant accuses himself, but by keeping the accusation self-directed, he avoids the judgment others could pronounce after having overheard the monologue. The idea is to force others to follow his example so that all confessants can become One, with Clamence as Judge and Penitent Superior. Clamence's motivations have changed but his actions and self-love have remained as they always were. He tells his listener: "I bend, because I continue to love myself. For example, after all I have told you, what do you think I developed? An aversion for myself? Come, come, it was especially with others that I was fed up. To be sure I knew my failings and regretted them. Yet I continued to forget them with meritorious obstinacy. The prosecution of others, on the contrary, went on constantly in my heart" (76). And later on in the monologue Clamence admits: "I haven't changed my way of life; I continue to love myself and to make use of others. Only, the confession of my crimes allows me to begin again lighter in heart and to taste a double enjoyment, first of my nature and secondly of a charming repentance" (142). As a judge Clamence used to set himself above everyone; as a judge-penitent he does the same. This is Clamence's solution, but he is not happy with it. It is the life of a man who has been banished forever from the paradise of innocence—a state of unawareness of sin—and who, with malicious intent, seeks a following to make his new life worthwhile. Clamence no longer lives in Eden where there existed, as William R. Mueller commented, "the freedom to give rather than to receive, the freedom to judge rather than be judged."[13] With the responsibility for his own actions, Clamence has now begun the search for a method to avoid being judged. This is accomplished by turning people into penitents who acknowledge their own wrong doings, and next become their own judge. Clamence's confession has the main purpose of forcing the listener into self-recognition during the cynical account of sneering self-contempt. "The more I accuse myself, the more I have a right to judge you. Even better, I provoke you into judging yourself, and this relieves me of that much of the burden" (140). The discontented, still unaware of their perverted condition, he converts to his way of thinking to acquire company in the pact for the preservation of the Fall. He has one certainty which he preaches: since Adam's exile is everlasting, a future Utopia of autonomous Dictatorship of Guilt is the sole remaining promise.

On a whole it is not so easy to determine what kind of person Clamence really is. The judge-penitent admits this himself: "It's very hard to disentangle the true from the false in what I am saying" (119). Serious intent and irony overlap in Clamence's confession. Several critics agree that to greater or lesser extents Camus himself, as well as his quarrel with Sartre and Existentialism, appears thinly disguised in various passages of the *récit*. "It is not unlikely," Carl Viggiani writes, "that *La Chute* is a product of a profound moral crisis in Camus. There are so many thinly veiled autobiographical facts in the narrative that Camus' image can be seen fairly clearly behind that of his judge-penitent."[14] Others back this argument.[15] The possibility is certainly not excluded because the *récit* is, among other aspects, an attack upon the thought of the day.

The Fall was originally intended as one of the stories to be included in *Exile and the Kingdom* (1957), and Brée, placing it within the context of the collection, compares it with "The Renegade,"[16] also a monologue that deals with fallen man. With the fact that these pieces of writing are monologues, there is an indication of the main characters' isolation: they are figures who have seen through the irresponsibility of their earlier ideals and who have been converted to faithful slaves of an available totalitarian system. Perhaps they are "the modern intellectuals" who wish for death or seek a tyranny to endure.[17] Regardless of whether the interpretation is thus applied, the fact remains that Clamence and the Renegade are a danger to their fellow men, the former still in theory, the latter already a physical threat. The Renegade, the tongueless missionary, has already been converted by the cruel sungod of the desert to serve the brutes of the salt empire. Clamence, the false prophet, seeks to bring people together for an alliance of consolidated guilt.

Both the narratives try to puncture the fake ideal of security in
a reasoned welfare, especially that of the existentialists who, in
fear of the individual, support the totalitarian religion of the
proletariat, that is, communism. *The Fall* could be called an
attack upon the guilt feelings of the educated bourgeoisie who
escape in a calculated risk the threat of freedom for the slavery
of mass sentiment. Anne Minor's discussion of *Exile and the
Kingdom* is appropriate in this regard. "The Renegade" she
sees as the reflection of a tragic era in which, "For Camus, the
'knight of the absurd,' it is better to face absurdity in the name
of revolt than bow down to evil in the name of logic. Whatever
the drama of absurdity may be, that of the logic of evil is
worse."[18]

In *The Fall* Camus writes an ironic protest against this by
caricaturing a reasonable man. Camus, unlike his character
Clamence, does not find man guilty. He has stated earlier in
The Myth of Sisyphus that a mind "imbued with the absurd"
realizes that "there may be responsible persons" but that "there
are no guilty ones."[19] In an interview of years later Franck
Jotterand asked Camus: "What do you think of this assertion
that we are all guilty?" The answer was: "Many modern
authors, including the atheistic existentialists, have eliminated
God; but they have preserved the idea of original sin. The
innocence of creation has been overasserted. Today, the idea
is to crush us under the weight of our guilt. There is, I believe,
an intermediate truth."[20] From this interview at the time that
The Fall was being planned, it can be deduced that Camus still
believed in the guilt of the Creator who punishes mankind for
Adam's rebellion. But God should not carry all the blame; man
shares the responsibility. It may be said that Camus looked for
the truth by distorting the case in *The Fall* in depicting an advocate of man's guilt in bold outline.

In *The Fall* man is to be blamed. Clamence is a frightened
man, ready to do anything to escape his self-accusation. He
lives in a seedy city, "the mark of a world that has seen better
days," "an ancient image, the image of despair and disintegration in Isaiah and Jeremiah."[21] He is cut off from the cosmos in
the prison of civilization, and he suggests a way out by proposing a return to pre-Christian days of judgment without

Mercy.[22] Clamence is abandoned to the Christian tradition of the West. He stands in history and, unlike the stranger Meursault, he tries to save his skin by avoiding the accusation and judgment of the totalitarian state at large. He is the living proof of Camus' thesis in *The Rebel* (1951) that a dictatorship of the majority *must* flourish in a post-Christian world.

Even though man's guilt feelings are being exaggerated with heavy irony, a new and definite view of man appears in the *récit*. In *The Plague* "la condition humaine" was attacked by the plague from without; in *The Fall* its festering presence comes from within, brought out into the open by Clamence. He is a scourge, the plague personified, and as such the prophet of corruption. In *The Plague* Camus gave the roles of Goodness to the major characters, cowardice and treachery in the face of danger had only walk-on parts. There is Cottard who enjoys the state of plague because it plunges everyone into the same plight of condemnation; as Tarrou records it: "The thing he'd most detest is being cut off from others; he'd rather be one of a beleaguered crowd than a prisoner alone. . . . We have no police nowadays; no crimes past or present, no more criminals —only condemned men hoping for the most capricious of pardons."[23] This attitude of Cottard, comments André Nicolas, "has served as basic theme for *The Fall*; Clamence, after having become aware of the impurity of his intentions, wants to lead all mankind astray within their awareness of guilt. It is a means of leaving solitude, but it presupposes nihilism."[24] It seems very likely that the motivations of Cottard functioned as fundamental theme. However, the attitude of the personified Plague in *State of Siege* (1948) is another interesting basis for the attitude in Clamence's pose. The last speech before the curtain falls on the first part of the play Camus gave to The Plague. On the *highest* point of the palace he stands and proclaims: "I am the ruler here; this is a fact, therefore it is a right. A right that admits of no discussion; a fact that you must accept. . . . I prefer to look like a quite ordinary person. . . . That's one of my ways of vexing you, and being vexed will do you good; you still have much to learn." All sentiment will go by the board, The Plague continues, and organizations will replace it. Death will be statistically determined and badges will be worn, indicating "marked down for elimination." "So the others, people who think these marks are no concern of theirs . . . will treat you as suspects and edge away from you. But you need not feel aggrieved; these marks concern them also, they're all down on our lists and nobody is overlooked. In fact all are suspects—that's the long and the short of it. . . . I bring you order, silence, total justice. I don't ask you to thank me for this; it's only natural, what I am doing here for you. Only, I must insist on your collaboration. My administration has begun."[25] This conclusion is as somber and frightening as that of *The Fall*: "But let's not worry! It's too late now. It will always be too late. Fortunately!" (147). In *The Plague* this acknowledgment was still overshadowed by the novel's conclusion that there are more things to admire in men than to despise. Here as well as in *The Rebel* the emphasis falls on an accused God and a natural innocence of man which allows for their solidarity. Solitary existence is a theme of *The Fall*.

Man's state of isolation is a direct result of the Fall: upon birth he enters a world of sin. Christianity has kept man aware of this and has developed within its believers a feeling of guilt which requires penance. *The Fall* is an attack upon this pervasive feeling of guilt and the recognition of man's responsibility in having contributed to this condition in the name of God and country. By doing so Camus experiments within Christian tradition.

The frame of the novel is derived from Christianity. The theme of the book is the Fall and its hero is Clamence, an exiled Adam, who lives in Hell—a condition reminiscent of Sartre's *No Exit* and Eliot's *The Cocktail Party* in which hell is being oneself, alone among others. To Camus Amsterdam is the infernal pit, the center of Dante's hell, enclosed by the concentric circles of the canals.[26] Within these confines (including the isle of Marken which lies just off the coast in the Zuyder Zee) Clamence moves about as a guide. Leon S. Roudiez keenly observed that the narrator of *The Fall* is "a modern travesty of Vergil," a figure who "had been erroneously considered as a prophet of the coming of Christ."[27] Appropriately, the false prophet for post-World-War-II times lives in what was once the Jewish neighborhood, a historical site of recent suffering and destruction. Here he gathers his strength to speak about the history of Christian civilization. His name, Jean-Baptiste Clamence, John the Baptist of Clemency, is polemically directed against Christianity. He proclaims everything but Grace. The doves, symbols of peace and innocence, circle the Dutch skies, unable to come down because there is "never a head on which to light" (73). Yet, the doves never leave the sky. When Clamence notices that they are gathering at nightfall, he calls the moment sinister.[28] He feels that the Holy Ghost is not wanted among his followers, those who "rush out to build piles of faggots to replace churches," and who "believe solely in sin, never in grace" (135).

At the conclusion of the *récit* snow begins to fall. As Clamence watches the illusion of purity, he turns to his listener: "It must be the doves, surely. . . . What an invasion. . . . Everyone will be saved, eh?—and not only the elect" (145). His believing companion is victimized. Clamence enjoys the success of his role as false diviner and suggests: "From today on you will sleep every night on the ground for me" (145). All those who acknowledge his reality must be ready to bow down to him. Clamence's triumph is as malignant as original sin—it perpetuates the feelings of guilt and denies any mercy of judgment. It shows the inability to believe in God and the refusal to believe in Grace.

Although God is excluded from Clamence's world, the Christ of the New Testament holds an important place in his awareness. He admires him as the Just Man who was betrayed by Christianity. He who preached love was condemned by the people and later made divine. Christ was "ordained of God," says Peter, "to be the Judge of quick and dead"—a message so important that the Holy Ghost falls "on all them which heard the word."[29] Today people are judged in His name by members of a Church founded on a coward called Peter, who denied Him three times. Christ made a play on words, Clamence thinks, when he called Peter the "rock," and added, "upon which I will build my church." Surely, "irony could go no further" (116). If then our faith in justice is but a parody of the divine intent, we should be satisfied with the solution Clamence proposes: the coming of a judging savior who can promote a solidarity based on fear.

Clamence has recognized in Christ the man who accomplished what he has been unable to bring about. Both are aware of man's guilt of which they are a part. Christ lived with the shared guilt in the murder of Rachel's children, much as Rieux lived with his helplessness to prevent the death of Oran's children. Both Christ and the doctor heard the weeping voices of the mothers to remind them that they were alive. Clamence has heard of sorrow also, but he uses it against people by convincing them that this is the natural condition of man in an evil world. He cannot give up the only thing he knows: "Knowing what he knew, familiar with everything about man—ah, who would have believed that crime consists less in making others die than in not dying oneself!" (113). Christ let himself be crucified in order not to be an accomplice in the wickedness of the time. There is no salvation possible. His desolateness and His fear of death show at the cross: "My God, my God, why hast thou forsaken me?" This cry of agony might have warned people of the void behind the painted veil of life. But the liar was succeeded by the censor. Luke, the third recorder of the life of Christ, left these words out and so distorted the truth. Christ has left this world to its own, false devices "to carry on, whatever happens, even when we are lodged in the little-ease, knowing in turn what he knew, but incapable of doing what he did and of dying like him" (114). Christ was the first of the Just to be destroyed by a sense of guilt and the nonexistence of reconciliation.

In order to compare the position of Clamence with what Christians consider to be the fall of man, one might consider *The Fall* to be a paraphrase of Genesis 3. The consequence of Clamence's fall are much like those of Adam and Eve who, wanting to be like God, aspired to know both good and evil. They wanted to rid themselves of dependence upon God in order to match His ability to judge in an autonomous state. When they ate of the fruit, their capacity to judge became directed at themselves: they discovered they were naked. The observation destroyed their natural unity of sexuality, and with it other natural relationships were destroyed in their new, autonomous judgment. Suddenly man found himself faced with, instead of one with, his fellow man, his work, and Nature. Danger and death became known within this unity-severed awareness. This disruption of natural relationships may well be designated with the concept of original sin. This break is the immediate consequence of the offense against God, the Father. Those who cut off this communion also alienate themselves from all those made in His image. The lawlessness which resulted from the Patricide led to the fratricide of Genesis 4.

Camus' opinion of Cain does not coincide with this Christian interpretation. In *The Rebel* it is stated that Cain's crime is a retaliation of God's crime: the refusal to accept Cain's offering in preference to Abel's. It is right, however, that Cain wanted to appropriate divine right by wanting to become God. This desire was natural in man's new state inherited from Adam and Eve. Cain was born outside the paradise of innocence in the land of banishment. Fallen man is a judge in his autonomy, and as judge he has separated himself from his communion with men. He discards his neighbor and is thereby himself discarded. "In that the children of Cain have triumphed, increasingly, throughout the centuries, the God of the Old Testament can be said to have been incredibly successful. Paradoxically, the blasphemers have injected new life into the jealous God whom Christianity wished to banish from history. One of their most profoundly audacious arts was to recruit Christ into their camp by making His story end on the Cross and on the bitter note of the cry that precedes His agony. By this means it was possible to preserve the implacable face of a God of hate."[30] Until Dostoevsky and Nietzsche rebellion is directed against the cruel divinity, Camus goes on, but once God was found dead in the mind and heart of man and the divinity of Christ denied, there was nothing left to love or hate in particular. Commenting on Nietzsche, Camus finds that "Deprived of the divine will, the world is equally deprived of unity and finality. That is why it is impossible to pass judgment on the world. Any attempt to apply a standard of values to the world leads finally to a slander on life. Judgments are based on what is, with reference to what should be—the kingdom of heaven, eternal concepts, or moral imperatives. But what should be does not exist; and the world cannot be judged in the name of nothing."[31] As Camus sees it, the world must be judged in the name of something. Yet, we need a point of reference, and to establish this we set ourselves up as standard for judgment. We thus arrive at the fictional character of Clamence.

Camus' narrator knows that man has continued to live in a fallen state without hope. There was a brief respite during the three years Christ taught, but those who came after Him falsified His teachings and examples. They became false prophets, and Clamence feels himself to be their natural heir. What Camus conceives Clamence's particular fall to be is hard to say. Perhaps Cruickshank was right when he wrote, "Man is seen more as continually falling than fallen,"[32] an observation plausible within the pessimistic context of the *récit*. It is clear that the scene on the bridge and the derisive laughter of the conscience are only revelations of an already existing condition. When Clamence is shaken out of his complacent happiness, he becomes aware that he had already fallen as lawyer, as concentration camp pope, and as lover. Because of this uncertainty the time of the Fall cannot be recalled, and it is difficult to say what the basis of his guilt might be; therefore, it cannot be held either that Clamence is solely responsible for his loss of grace. He fell with mankind as accomplice.

Whatever the fall may have been, the consequences for Clamence are that from having been a lawyer he has become a judge. From a solitary defender he has turned into a solitary man-god. As a fallen man, as a judge, he has followed Cain into exile to lead a shadowy existence in Limbo-on-the-North-Sea watching the traffic on the canals.

Clamence spies on the misfortunes of others to find the guilty lives on which to live. He forces the victims into penance by judging them, and like a prophet he feels that he is doing right because he has been "really called" (84) to be a judge-penitent. In earlier days he had already been self-elected pope over people whose suffering he shared. This was his position in the camp in Tripolis where he held the power of life and death over the people who trusted him. With Clamence we find the confirmation of Camus' thesis in *The Rebel* that a man who no longer believes in God feels the need to become a godhead because he cannot and dares not live with the limitations of being merely man. The man who has eliminated God's presence feels his weakness and to invoke power he appoints himself to be his own godhead's representative on earth and thus becomes a danger to mankind. As an authoritarian he crawls into the system which relieves him of responsibility. The judge becomes the prisoner and the slave to the cause which hides him. Not the man but the system becomes the divine substitute. This central thought of *The Rebel* appears in Christian framework in *The Fall* and coincides with most of Genesis 3. The difference lies in the uncertainty of the origin of Clamence's fall and the utter lack of eventual salvation for Clamence or anyone else under the spell of his false prophecies.

The isolation in which Clamence finds himself is inviolable because he will not consider relinquishing his autonomy. He cannot join another being, let alone abandon himself to someone. He desires communion and love but is incapable of fulfilling this desire. "It seems to me that at that time I felt the need of love. Obscene, isn't it?" (99). When the plague of destruction comes from within, man is divided unto himself. His guilt makes him narcissistic and egocentric. It is in this aspect that Clamence resembles his predecessor Caligula in the play Camus wrote during World War II. Both turn away from love once they have left the paradise of innocence behind them. Rather than exert themselves in understanding mankind and themselves through love, they assume the world to be evil and contribute to it so they may rise as an absolute power of Satanic magnitude. What Rachel Bespaloff said of Caligula also holds for Clamence: "He wants to be guilty; he needs the transgression of sacrilege in order to assert his freedom. And at the same time, with all his might, he denies his guilt, for indeed, what justice would there be under the rule of equivalence? He externalizes evil in order to liberate himself, and by doing so he clings to necessity and plays into its hands. The externalizing of evil is nothing but a way of shifting the responsibility for original sin on an absent god."[33] Clamence needs the freedom of "heights." He seeks it to avoid the judgment others might pronounce upon him. He is the "comedian" in sackcloth who pronounces a fake judgment on his own actions to forestall others, because once the world turns upon him he will lose his autonomous state. Clamence clings to the necessity to externalize evil to maintain the status quo of comparison with others. So long as we have this chance, we escape a final judgment. Beware the Last Judgment, "It takes place every day" (111). Clamence is constantly on the alert: the Judgment would be terrifying if there were no method of gauging the extent of one's guilt. When man stands alone, guilt has become an absolute state in which he ceases to be.

Clamence cannot believe in reconciliation, and the extent to which he needs to play the false prophet is indicated by his confession of hiding a stolen painting. For safekeeping he received one day a panel of Van Eyck's altarpiece "L'Agneau mystique" called "Les Juges intègres." The thief has never been found and the painting never traced to Clamence. The custodians of the cathedral at Ghent eventually replaced the original with an accurate copy. To Clamence it is important that no one has been able to tell the copy from the original; because in this way he continues to dominate. He is the only one who knows where the true "Just Judges" are and, more importantly, *who* they are. Clamence remarks that the judges on the panel he owns move toward the Sacred Animal, the Divine Lamb whose innocence no longer exists: "This way everything is in harmony. Justice being definitively separated from innocence—the latter on the cross and the former in the cupboard. I have the way clear to work according to my convictions" (130). Today the false judges move toward the Lamb in Ghent, and Clamence is their accomplice in keeping silent. Because of him, justice and salvation remain separate. The world continues to await the judgment of the absent True Judges whom Clamence hides in the closet.

Deception is what Clamence needs in order to continue his mission. He has always had that prized ability to lead people with an air of benign indifference. In his early Parisian days he was the ideal heir of Camus' earth at Tipasa (*Noces*, 1937), aware of a harmony within him. He did well: he brought a semblance of unity, through justice, to the dispossessed who seek refuge in civilization. He was the superman people needed to believe in, needed to recognize as their rescuer: "People thought they had met me before" (28). Clamence grows accustomed to the role he is forced to play and, exulting in the newly found power, he begins to imagine himself "a king's son or a burning bush" (29). He feels that he has the stature of Moses with a voice like God's.

After his fall, having seen in Djemila, the land on the other side of the Tipasa hills, his own destructibility, Clamence loses his conviction of harmony. He adopts the role of comedian to advocate a false desert state, a Promised Land of suspended salvation. He turns to all those who, like him, have been cast out of Eden. They are the people who want a prophet and as Clamence notices: "Something must happen—and that explains most human commitments. Something must happen, even loveless slavery" (37). They want only to escape from their solitary state. Prophets live by words and zeal; their success depends upon divine recognition. Since Clamence knows that the world is without God, he proceeds cautiously: "I progressed on the surface of life, in the realm of words as it were, never in reality" (50). The words attracted people; they came and wanted to cling, but there was no confirmation to cling to: no Holy Ghost, no flaming chariot as token of divine intent. Waiting for the sign, people continue to flock toward Clamence. He enjoys it: "I could live happily only on condition that all the individuals on earth, or the greatest possible number, were turned toward me, eternally in suspense, devoid of independent life, and ready to answer my call at any moment" (68). Clamence is now prepared, in Brée's words, "to fill the world with his own image."[34] Having become a godhead, he is ready to accuse the whole human race and heaven itself. Like John the Baptist he has come to the realization that his strength lies in his scorn, and that, like God, he is present without being there: "I was absent at the moment when I took up the most space" (87).

Toward the end of the confession a weary Clamence admits to the desperation which prompted his willing ascent to the leadership of the guilty: "In solitude and when fatigued, one is after all inclined to take oneself for a prophet. When all is said and done, that's really what I am, having taken refuge in a desert of stone, fogs, and stagnant water—an empty prophet for shabby times, Elijah without a messiah" (117). Clamence acknowledges that the belief in grace for him and for all those in his situation is but a temptation. His universe is entire unto itself and his guilt is defined by this universe: he is guilty because he failed in what he expected himself to do. His own norms were the judge and not, as in Christianity, the breaking of a covenant with God and God's creation.

Clamence refuses forgiveness of sins, grace, and salvation from outside as obstinately as Camus turned down eternal life in *The Myth of Sisyphus*. Camus refused in order to remain faithful to *this* life; Clamence refuses salvation in the name of his type of justice and for the sake of his only life, unworthy as it may be. For him it is too late forever. Only one value remains: pride in being an example of righteousness. Just imagine, he suggests to the listener, that you would report me for having hidden a stolen painting. If you did, I would be betrayed and perhaps become a martyr. "I would be decapitated. . . . Above the gathered crowd you would hold up my still warm head, so that they could recognize themselves in it and I could again dominate—an exemplar. All would be consummated; I should have brought to a close, unseen and unknown, my career as a false prophet crying in the wilderness and refusing to come forth" (146–147). Until that day, however, he shall continue to play at being god. Unseen and unknown like his dead Lord, God the Father, he watches the multitudes of the Last Judgment ascend toward him to hand them testimonials of bad character and habit. Clamence is caught in the universe of his own ego, which he has filled with his image. He is to remain in the "malconfort" of exemplar until his death. What is to happen to his followers and how the world must cope with their festering presence Camus has left deliberately unresolved.

4

Dostoevsky's
The Possessed

ALBERT CAMUS WAS INFLUENCED BY FYODOR DOS-
toevsky, a fact Brée and Cruickshank in their full-length studies of the French author have already pointed out.[1] Starting with
Camus' own admissions, they have drawn legitimate parallels
in comparative studies. To mention one similarity: in the
work of both we find the theme of murder and, in particular,
reflections on patricide. Camus followed Dostoevsky in *The
Stranger* when he had Meursault say: "All normal people . . .
had more or less desired the death of those they loved, at some
time or another."[2] Ivan Karamazov is more specific yet when
he accuses everyone: "They all desire the death of their fa-
thers."[3] Those who do cannot adjust to the world's injustice
for which they hold a father figure responsible.

In particular the theological aspect of patricide is stated and
evaluated in the work of both authors. It is God, the Father,
the Creator, who is responsible for a world in which children
suffer and die. Ivan's refusal to accept the torture of innocent
creatures as part of an Inspired and Harmonious Design is a
central thought to *The Plague* and *The Just Assassins*. When
Alyosha speaks of God's omniscience, Ivan retorts: "All I know
is that there is suffering and that there are none guilty."[4] On
these grounds man rebels against God, and on this anguished

reply of Ivan is based the second part of *The Rebel*. Both
Camus and Dostoevsky knew an all-pervasive love for life.
"I've asked myself many times," Ivan says to Alyosha,
"whether there is in the world any despair that would over-
come this frantic thirst for life. . . . I have a longing for life,
and I go on living in spite of logic. Though I may not believe
in the order of the universe, yet I love the sticky little leaves
as they open in spring. I love the blue sky. I love some people."[5]
The dying Ippolyt, explaining his actions to the "idiot" prince,
states this love for life explicitly: "It's life that matters, nothing but life—the process of discovering, the everlasting and
perpetual process, not the discovery itself, at all."[6] It is a question central to Camus' work which, as with Dostoevsky, re-
ceives an affirmative reply. For Camus life even has a value
which makes him qualify Ivan's premise that if there were no
immortality, nothing "would be immoral, everything would
be lawful, even cannibalism."[7] Camus observes, " 'Everything
is permitted' does not mean that nothing is forbidden."[8]

   The Fall, both in form and content, has been influenced by
the confessional, first-person narrative *Notes from Underground* and by "At Tihon's" ("Stavrogin's Confession") from
The Possessed. With regard to the content it is especially true
for the Dostoevskian motif of the painting which for Clamence
has symbolic significance. In *The Possessed*, and in *The Idiot*
as well, there are paintings which are of decisive importance to
the main characters. Furthermore, there is a love for nature,
an antirationalism, a glorification of one's own land and people,
and an opposition to the spirit of Western Europe—all these are
points of correspondence between Camus and Dostoevsky.

   In *The Possessed* Camus has seen one of the "most profound" expressions of "our historical destiny."[9] He agreed
with the Russian writer that it is necessary to ask the question
the man-god poses, but he differs with the final answer given
in *The Brothers Karamazov*. Camus feels that Kirillov's sacrifice was negated by Alyosha's comment to the children that men
will meet again in an afterlife. Dostoevsky, just before his
death, made the Kierkegaardian leap and so "continued to
cherish" mankind's "blind hopes."[10] In spite of all similarity
there is a clear distinction in the two authors' affirmation and

denial of the Christian faith. In one of the most pertinent comparative studies Jacques Madaule sees the relationship between the religious attitudes of Camus and Dostoevsky as follows:

> They are both preoccupied with atheism, but not at all in the same way. For Dostoevsky it is a battle at the very heart of the self, fought every moment against the temptation of atheism and not to cease until death, because "if God does not exist, everything is permitted." . . . Camus' atheism is an acquired fact. One does not even question it. It is. Within Camus' work the characters are atheistic as simply as they breathe. . . . Dostoevsky's atheistic heroes are the unhappy ones. Their liver never ceases to be devoured on the mountainside of a spiritual Caucasus. On the other hand, Camus' characters, such as Dr. Rieux, are heroes in the proper sense of the word. They deem themselves to be under an even greater obligation because God does not exist.[11]

Kirillov, the man for whom atheism was an "acquired fact," held great fascination for Camus. In *The Myth of Sisyphus* there is a special essay devoted to him as one of Dostoevsky's important spokesmen. Already in a *Carnet* entry for December 1938, Camus had agreed with this fictional hero that to commit suicide is to prove one's freedom. In a later entry—a letter dated September 24, 1944—Camus was still fascinated with Kirillov's theories. Indeed, he notes, the only way to create God is to become him: the proof lies in the whole history of Western civilization.[12]

In 1959 Camus finally completed the adaptation of *The Possessed* for the stage. For five years he had worked on it, and for almost twenty years he claims to have taken "sustenance" from this novel as a "prophetic book," "not only because it prefigures our nihilism, but also because its protagonists are torn or dead souls unable to love and suffering from that inability, wanting to believe and yet unable to do so." Camus ends this "Foreword" to his stage adaptation by introducing the play's subject: "the murder of Shatov" and "the death of Stavrogin, a contemporary hero."[13] The play was well received in Paris and, according to Warren Ramsey, it is "a powerful play remarkably faithful to the novel."[14] Kirillov has been given a minor part in keeping with Dostoevsky's fictional world: the bizarre superman is an important, but only occasional presence. The role of protagonist has been assigned to Nikolay Stavrogin, the false emissary from primordial chaos, who is without belief in life or death. Ramsey's review holds that Stavrogin, as a character on stage, has lost his air of mystery and has come into the foreground as an "all-too-human nobleman."[15] This may be true; however, it is not evident from reading the play, which can well prove that Stavrogin, like Jean-Baptiste Clamence, is most effective as an evil force when he is but a disembodied presence. Dostoevsky was certainly aware—as his *Notebook* indicates—of this possibility when, rather than building a drama around Stavrogin, he created a novel to contain the unseen diffusion of a spirit-laming pestilence. The finished work partakes of both genres.

As expected, *The Possessed* lent itself well to a stage adaptation. It is not surprising, because the novel consists mainly of recorded conversations with characters continuously joining in or taking leave. Any action that takes place—with some nonessential exceptions—is confined to a room in someone's house or an area outdoors bordered by walls, fences, or railings. The time elapsed appears as a perpetual moment, apart from conventional time. Throughout the narrative the words flow from day into night, and the fact that the actual events which take place in the novel last two weeks is blurred by the constant exchange of ideas and opinions. The second and decisive appearance of Stavrogin at his mother's and his visits to his friends that night occur within twenty-four hours. Eight days elapse and the climactic grand ball finally takes place. The morning's preparation, the disastrous gathering, and the murderous aftermath take but forty-eight hours.[16] The remaining incidents are covered in the introductory exposition and epilogue-like conclusion for which Dostoevsky employed a narrator, a neutral observer whose "chronicle" could also serve to provide for necessary transitions.

Joseph W. Beach has written an excellent essay on the "dramatic tendency" in Dostoevsky, in which he discusses the "single center of interest" essential to drama, the "limitation of place," the "amount of time covered," and the "developments" within a single day.[17] Another commentator, Vyacheslav Ivanov, speaks of the essential law of tragedy, which partakes of "epic rhythm" and the "progressively gathering momentum of events." Further he comments on Dostoevsky's "cruel Muse," tragic "to the last degree," who brings about a "catharsis" through fear and pity. Ivanov considers Dostoevsky's dramatic technique in fiction commendable, but not without fault: distracting, for example, is the artificial juxtaposition of character and event in the same place and time.[18] George Steiner, like Beach and Ivanov, discusses the elements of place and time; but then he goes on to mention the "essential structure of dialogue" expanded by "stage-directions" into a novel.[19] What Constantin Motchoulski had to say about "le dramatisme de Dostoievski" can be well applied to *The Possessed*: it is a three-act "novel-tragedy," "a theatre of tragic masks," with, at the end, a stage littered with corpses.[20]

Within this theatrical and tragic world Dostoevsky depicted a contemporary hero whose amoral actions and casual advice destroyed the people around him. Stavrogin is admired. He lives on solitary heights. Discontented intellectuals and members of the avant-garde bourgeoisie idolize him. He is feared by those who have met with his malicious indifference and hated by those whose innocence withstands his perversion. He brings about pity and fear in those who watch him or come under his influence; and together with his fictional audience the reader is drawn into the timeless universe of chaos. With a horrid fascination Stavrogin's circle is attracted by his "melodious" voice and discomforting silences to be destroyed against a wall of indifference. Prior to the action described in the novel, Stavrogin is said to have suggested ideas to others with which they can sustain faith. Once he enters the fictional framework, his former followers come back, and now Stavrogin refuses to acknowledge his earlier words. All those who become involved in such a confrontation resent doubting the integrity of the Master. They want a clear answer, and in their persistence they are drawn into a web of conspiracy to betray and destroy mankind. It is this destruction, this "monstrous a villainy" of violence against others and against self which Dostoevsky intended to present as a warning to the times.

In my novel *The Possessed* I made the attempt to depict the
manifold and heterogeneous motives which may prompt even
the purest of heart and the most naive people to take part in the
perpetration of so monstrous a villainy. The horror lies precisely in the fact that in our midst the filthiest and most villain-
ous act may be committed by one who is not a villain at all!
This, however, happens not only in our midst but throughout
the world; it has been so from time immemorial, during transitional epochs, at times of violent commotion in people's lives
—doubts, negations, scepticism and vacillation regarding the
fundamental social convictions. . . . The possibility of considering oneself not as a villain, and sometimes almost not being one, while perpetrating a patent and incontestable villainy
—therein is our present-day calamity.[21]

In these "epochs" men fall in love with an advocate of nothingness; they want anarchy for anarchy's sake because it is the
only concrete and identifiable norm left. They lack all guiding
force, and they seek a leader to show them salvation. The
political theorist Shigalov, with whose work Stavrogin is familiar, anticipates Ivan Karamazov's "Grand Inquisitor" in
his discussion of equality. Men should be made slaves, and
Stavrogin is prompted to become their "director." Shigalov's
spokesman insists: "All are slaves and equal in their slavery. . . .
Slaves are bound to be equal. There has never been either freedom or equality. . . . Slaves must have directors. Absolute sub-
mission, absolute loss of individuality, but once in thirty years
Shigalov would let them have a shock and they would all suddenly begin eating one another up, to a certain point, simply
as a precaution against boredom." The leader for the West
shall be the Pope, the destroyer of Christ's teachings, and for
Russia there shall be Stavrogin: "You shall be for us," you
shall be the "idol" and the "sun" (II, viii, 424–425). But Stavrogin, with his usual phlegmatic attitude, refuses the honor.

Stavrogin's indifference is interpreted by his audience as a
sign of greatness and mystery, as a promise of salvation to
come. Stavrogin is an enigma to his fictional world and to his
readers. In order to solve the problem many critics attempt to
relate him to one or another of the archetypal heroes of literature. Vycheslav Ivanov finds the story of Stavrogin to be parallel to the Faust myth with the distinction, however, that the
hero, unlike Faust who is Satan's debtor, is the "vassal" of the

Tempter.[22] George Steiner sees in Dostoevsky's hero a "variant on the Satanic heroes of Byronism and the Gothic" and notes, moreover, that, like Antichrist, he "resembles the true Messiah."[23] Robert Payne finds religious overtones when he describes the hero as "the burning satanic core at the heart of things," "the Fallen Angel who wanders disconsolately through the world."[24] Lastly there are those who approach *The Possessed* in search of myth and archetypal pattern without specifically focusing on Stavrogin.[25] Generally, critics, in considering Dostoevsky's hero, speak of him as a man tormented by the demon of pride, suffering from estrangement, and living "below, not beyond, good and evil."[26] Stavrogin spreads chaos wherever he goes: "Wrapped in indifference, lost in an egotism he does not value, he passes by, simply but deadly, as if he were the inhabitant of another planet, spreading around him, impassively, a miasma as he goes."[27]

If commentators have been noticing all the varied directions for interpretation, they have concurred with Dostoevsky's attempt to create a tragic hero cloaked in mystery. When the author was still working on the novel, he wrote to his publisher Katkov (October 8, 1870) that the political agitator who had been intended as the main character was going to be replaced by another "Hauptperson," another central figure. "This other character in the novel (Nikolay Stavrogin) is also darkly suspicious; he is an evildoer. Nevertheless, I consider him a tragic figure. . . . Only one thing I want to note: this character I will depict only through scenes and actions, not through discursive argument; thus I hope that a distinctive individual will come to the fore."[28] This new hero had already been sketched on the pages of the writer's *Notebook*. Part of the entry for August 16, 1869, reads as follows: "*The prince*, somber, passionate, of demonic and disorderly character. Without any moderation in regard to the supreme question to be or not to be? To live or to destroy oneself? He decides that to go on as in the past is an impossibility; he continues to act as before, continues to violate." Several paragraphs later Dostoevsky reminds himself: "Everything is within the character of Stavrogin. Stavrogin ALL."[29] Since he is everything, he is part of the chaos in which he lives: "A depraved aristocrat and nothing more.

Nothing but disorder."[30] Nevertheless, this must go unrecognized within the world of *The Possessed*. It is essential that he
is depicted "comme un homme *extraordinaire*"[31] in order to
catch the attention of those waiting to be united. Human relationships had been shattered after The Fall and, indecisively,
man has wandered, waiting for a saviour to lead him to the
promised land of harmony. In his *Diary* Dostoevsky remarked:
"Everybody segregates himself, keeps aloof from others. . . .
Former ties are being severed without regret and everybody
acts by himself, and in this alone does he find consolation. If
he doesn't act, he wishes he could act. True, a great many people are not starting anything and never will start; even so,
they are detached; they stand apart, staring at the empty spot
and idly waiting for something. We all are awaiting something."[32] In *The Possessed* everyone is "waiting for something"
in Stavrogin, but the difficulty is that their prophet-elect cannot fill the "empty spot"; he lives in a state of anticipation,
looking for something himself; he embodies various beliefs
for those around him but can find no fulfillment himself. When
he reappears at his mother's home, having traveled abroad, he
is received with "naive solemnity." "In all eyes fastened upon
him could be read eager anticipation. Nikolay at once wrapped
himself in the most austere silence, which, of course, gratified
everyone much more than if he had talked till doomsday. In a
word, he was a success, he was the fashion. . . . He was not
found cheerful company: 'a man who has been suffering; a
man not like other people; he has something to be melancholy
about.' Even the pride and disdainful aloofness for which he
had been so detested four years before were now liked and re-
spected" (II, iv, 304). The reader, like the society of the small
Russian town, becomes involved with Stavrogin's perversions
and crimes. Inveigled, one overlooks his depravity, his vicious
conduct, his outrages against society, and his disdain for conventional morality. His remarks that "good and evil really do
not exist" and are "but a prejudice" ("At Tihon's," 712), are
difficult to judge. Stavrogin, like Clamence, is a mirror in which
each can recognize his anxieties, his ambivalence, his guilt, and
his complicity in the perpetuation of the fraud of Christian
civilization. Yet, Stavrogin himself is empty and, hence, aloof

in personal commitments. He longs for something that will release him from his boredom, and this desire even manifests itself in a need to overstate his guilt in order to attract attention. Those who project themselves into Stavrogin's consciousness find that his haughty indifference is not self-consistent: he acts for the sake of appearance, yet aware of his ever-changing masquerade. Above all he lacks the essential worth by which man can transcend himself, the ability to love, which brings to mind Father Zossima's assertion in *The Brothers Karamazov*: "What is hell? I maintain that it is the suffering of being unable to love."[33] Surely, this is a state of being with which Stavrogin is familiar.

Nikolay hardly knew his parents and was raised by a tutor who taught the child to weep. This teacher succeeded in reaching the "deepest chords in his pupil's heart" and "aroused in him a first vague sensation of that eternal, sacred yearning which some elect souls can never give up for cheap gratification." The narrator of the novel further tells that the child left home, and soon took "to riotous living with a sort of frenzy," while "associating with the dregs of the population" (I, ii, 38–39). Apparently, the "yearning" has not been gratified. Stavrogin turns to debauchery, furiously joining the "mockery" of life. Like Camus' Caligula, he transcends all distinctions between good and evil and passes into the amorality of a realm where all actions are of equal value. Stavrogin has "outraged children" and has seen "no distinction in beauty between some brutal obscene action and any great exploit, even the sacrifice of life for the good of humanity." He has found "identical beauty, equal enjoyment in both extremes" (II, i, 257). At the conclusion of the novel, in a letter to the only woman who has understood him, Stavrogin writes: "I've tried the depths of debauchery and wasted my strength over it" (III, viii, 685), but he is still not sure why he followed this course.

Concurring with other critics,[34] Nicholas Berdyaev proposes a partial answer by suggesting a "defiant self-affirmation" which many Dostoevskian heroes have in common. In them is shown "freedom deteriorating into self-will and a defiant self-affirmation to be thenceforward ineffectual, worthless, and a

drain on the individual. . . . Freedom that is arbitrary destroys
itself. . . . Man is consumed as by fire amid the shadows of the
wilderness that he has himself chosen."[35] If in his self-will
Stavrogin is an enigma to himself, to others he often seems to
be a mask. The first time he sees Stavrogin, the narrator comments that he was "bold and self-reliant, as none of us were."
His appearance was impressively handsome, "yet at the same
time there seemed something repellent about him. It was said
that his face suggested a mask" (I, ii, 40–41). This question
of the mask, this unchanging, "quiet" expression, lends a
semblance of mysterious unity to an already fragmented personality. Several times Stavrogin is called "Prince"; but the
form of address, like the name Stavrogin (derived from the
Greek word for "cross," *stauros*), suggests the ironical attri-
butes of the deceptive mask the world sees. As the pretender
to the throne of chaos, he contains elements of charm and
grandeur; and his conspicuous appearance, like "a diamond
set in the dirty background of . . . life" (I, v, 187), draws people
to the edge of a barren wilderness.

The intense reaction induced by the presence or actions of
Stavrogin is one of fascination and fear, horror and admiration. He is the perfect decoy to draw mankind into the complicity of utter negation. When he appears, when he clashes
with others, when he is related to the past, participates in the
present, or projects himself into the future, awe or terror en-
velops his surroundings. Those who have felt the lash of his
malign indifference link him with the lower forms of animal
life: they see him as a viper, a spider, or a clawing beast.[36] His
presence incites the consciousness of evil, and only the Innocent
instinctively recognize the demonic. This intuitive perception
becomes evident when Stavrogin's wife, the cripple Marya,
says to him: "When I saw your mean face after I'd fallen down
and you picked me up—it was like a worm crawling into my
heart" (II, ii, 282). One night he goes to see Kirillov, who is
playing with a small child, held by a woman. After Stavrogin
had entered, "the child caught sight of him, nestled against
the old woman and went off into a prolonged infantile wail"
(II, i, 235). Yet no others reject him instinctively, and even
Marya has initially been captivated by her "savior." His con-

verts, who have elected him to fill the "empty spot" in their lives, regard him as their idol, their light and sun until the crucial moment when they are cast off to meet their fate in darkness.

At one time Stavrogin had given advice to those in need, but having returned to the family estate from St. Petersburg, he denies the validity of earlier advice by refusing to comment. Stavrogin has been made to recognize the futility of faith in people, in ideas, and in his own importance. In mankind's willing assent to believe in him and to serve his need Stavrogin has been offered a chance for self-exultation and so to rise above the masses. In the city he lived in the limelight of his power until the day when he raped a young girl and allowed her to hang herself afterwards in a delirium of guilt. For Stavrogin the concept of his superiority has collapsed with the realization that fear has entered his autonomous state. "The main thing was that I was afraid and that I was so conscious of being afraid. Oh, I know of nothing more absurd and more abominable! I had never experienced fear before, never before and never afterwards, but this one time in my life I was afraid, and in fact, I literally trembled. The intense consciousness of it was a profound humiliation" ("At Tihon's," 707). Stavrogin has been faced with the absurd in his recognition of the discrepancy between his actual self and the way he has conceived himself to be. Like Clamence who let a girl drown and then realized his vulnerability to judgment and condemnation, he runs from the confrontation only to meet, like Clamence, his baptism by absurdity. Dreaming of an "earthly paradise," he awakens, and while his eyes are still closed the image of the little girl shaking her fist at him throws its projection on the beauty of the earlier vision. "What I regret is not the crime, nor her death, I am not sorry for her, what I cannot bear is just that one instant, I can't, I can't, because I see her that way every day, and I know for a certainty that I am doomed" ("At Tihon's," 717). Stavrogin now returns to his ancestral estate to begin his life in the "malconfort" of guilt: in the "bird cage" (in "a small wooden box for starlings," the English meaning of Shvoreshniki, the Stavrogin estate) he begins his solitary exile.

Stavrogin is a netherworld incarnate. As an emissary of hell, he transmits a merciless spirit of destruction. Often he is present without being there: his shadow falls across all other characters. He remains unmovable within his own universe, and yet he is the force that initiates the deadly fate of those whom he encounters. Once these persons recognize him as a possible reality, their perdition becomes irrevocable. Stavrogin personifies all that is beyond hope and, hence, beyond human existence. He is not susceptible to thoughts or actions resulting from human passion: "Stavrogin would have shot his opponent in a duel . . . but it would have been without the slightest thrill of enjoyment, languidly, listlessly, even with *ennui* and entirely from unpleasant necessity." Granted, the narrator observes, he may feel anger under the circumstances, but it is "a calm, cold, if one may say so, *reasonable* anger," the "most terrible possible" (I, v, 206). His mother and Liza, the girl to whom he has been attracted for some time, realize the inhumanity of his being. Terror grips the mother when she intrudes upon her sleeping son "sitting strangely motionless." "His face was pale and forbidding, but it looked, as it were, numb and rigid. His brows were somewhat contracted and frowning. He positively had the look of a lifeless wax figure. . . . She withdrew on tiptoe . . . with a new oppression and a new anguish at her heart" (II, i, 232). Liza, after having spent the night with him, breaks out in terror: "I ought to confess that ever since those days in Switzerland I have had a strong feeling that you have something awful, loathsome, some bloodshed on your conscience, and yet something that would make you look very ridiculous" (III, iii, 534). Whatever the ridiculous has been, Liza voices her disappointment: "I always fancied that you would take me to some place where there was a huge wicked spider, big as a man, and we should spend our lives looking at it and being afraid of it. That's how our love would spend itself" (III, iii, 535). She does not realize that she has seen the spider of destruction, and she leaves the "bird cage" to meet her death. In *The Idiot* Dostoevsky employed a similar image to warn Ippolyt of the approach of the demon Rogozhin. In my delirium, Ippolyt says, "I seemed to fancy at times that I saw in some strange, incredible form that infinite Power, that dull, dark dumb force. I remember that someone seemed to lead me by the hand, holding a candle, to show me a huge and loathsome spider, and to assure me, laughing at my indignation, that this was that same dark, dumb and almighty power."[37]

This almighty power of diabolism pervades Dostoevsky's thinking, and as novelist he often depicts demonic powers. When the devil appears, he can do so in person, distinctly visible to a particular figure, as in the case of Ivan Karamazov and Ippolyt, or within another character as evil's advocate, which is the case with Stavrogin. In the first, Satan appears in a nightmare; in the second, evil is an intuitive reality.

When Ivan's devil wanders into his room, he acts like a "poor relative" in need of support. As an incarnation of Ivan he is "a phantom in life who has lost all beginning and end." Ivan wants to show him the door, but the devil clings to his "refuge" because he has found an advocate of the condition where "all things are lawful." This assumption has led the "visitor," who is always willing "to enter into the world" and to take a seat on a sofa, to give advice:

> I maintain that nothing need be destroyed, that we only need to destroy the idea of God in man, that's how we have to set to work. It's that, that we must begin with. Oh! blind race of men who have no understanding! As soon as men have all denied God . . . the old conception of the universe will fall of itself without cannibalism and what's more the old morality, and everything will begin anew. . . . Man will be lifted up with a spirit of divine Titanic pride and man-god will appear. . . . Even if this period never comes to pass, since there is anyway no God and no immortality, the new man may well become the man-god, even if he is the only one in the whole world. Promoted to his new position, he may light-heartedly overstep all the barriers of the old morality of the old slave-man.[38]

This quotation from *The Brothers Karamazov* throws light on Dostoevsky's earlier experimentation with Stavrogin in *The Possessed*. Contrary to Ivan, Stavrogin does not resist the temptation to "overstep all the barriers" and be lifted up with "Titanic pride." For Stavrogin God is dead so that for him there is nothing left to love or hate in particular. Stavrogin has removed himself to his lostness where his newly found isolation is inviolable. He is above and beyond human commitment:

in this lies his fascination for mankind, who wish to "catch" him so that they can believe in him. "To cook your hare you must first catch it, to believe in God you must first have a god" (II, i, 256). Stavrogin's own saying his followers remember.

Stavrogin is an alien in this world: "I'm an outsider, not your husband, nor your father, nor your betrothed," he says to his crippled wife (I, v, 184). One of his followers carefully reminds him during a discussion, "you see, I don't say 'our,' you don't like the word 'our,' I say *the* cause" (II, i, 227). To his "nurse" he writes: "I have no ties in Russia—everything is as alien to me there as everywhere" (III, viii, 685). Stavrogin has divorced himself from his native soil, and as Father Tihon reminds him: "One does not become a foreigner in one's own country with impunity." If one does, the punishment is boredom and idleness. Stavrogin is the epitome of disaffection with God and life, and he must suffer the woe of those "through whom temptation cometh" ("At Tihon's," 722).

The chapter of the novel "At Tihon's," in which Stavrogin confesses to the priest, is the first time[39] he shows a sincerity wrought in despair. However, as Tihon observes, the admission of sins may well be heavily dramatized and Stavrogin's desire for punishment yet another wish for self-assertion. "It is difficult for a man to take up his cross when he does not believe in the cross of Christ."[40] The narrator introduces the confession by observing that looking at the document he can sense a new, unexpected, and irreverent challenge to society. It is this, but it is also a turning point in the battle between "yearning" and resignation to Christianity. Stavrogin rejects the chance to practice humility and, as Father Tihon predicts, continues his search along a path of destruction.

Stavrogin himself relates that "I was so utterly bored that I could have hanged myself, and if I didn't, it was because I was still looking forward to something, as I have all my life" ("At Tihon's," 704–705). To relieve this boredom he first molests a child (explained away as a "psychological misunderstanding"), and, once the fear of discovery has passed, he again conceives the idea "of somehow crippling his life." He now decides to marry the lame Marya, who is not yet insane, "but simply a rapturous idiot." Yet, he admits: "I could never love anyone." Stavrogin's words speak for themselves, and the initial feeling of sympathy for his suffering soon turns to the awareness that one is in the presence of a liar seeking to be despised. As an exemplar of sin he wants to create a brotherhood of hate in which all can perish. " 'Perhaps I lied to you a good deal about myself,' Stavrogin repeated insistently. 'I myself do not know even yet. Well, what if I have defied them by the crudeness of my confession, if you *did* notice the challenge? That's the right way. They deserve it. I will only force them to hate me more, that's all. . . . I despise them all, just as I do myself, as much if not more, infinitely more. No one can be my judge' " ("At Tihon's," 723). Like Clamence, Stavrogin needs to preserve his eminent position in order not to perish in the judgment of the world. Tihon knows that the publication of the confession will destroy Stavrogin, not by the hate incited, but by the "laughter" over a fool who "kissed the nasty little girl's hand." "Who will understand the true reason for the confession? Indeed, people will purposely refuse to understand it, for such unconventional acts are feared; they rouse alarm . . . for the world loves its abomination and does not wish to see it threatened; for that reason people will turn it to ridicule, for ridicule is the world's strongest weapon" ("At Tihon's," 725). The priest succeeds in dissuading Stavrogin while realizing that the confessor will substitute crime for the publication. In accord with the prediction, Stavrogin becomes morally responsible for the deaths of many of the people who live under his dominance. He is guilty of Marya's murder in that, aware of its imminence, he takes no preventive steps. His failure to interfere is, in part, brought about by the vague hope that marrying Liza may bring what he has yearned for all his life. Liza, aware too late of having been implicated, goes to the scene of the crime and is lynched by the mob as "Stavrogin's woman." Moreover, as the idol of the revolutionary figures, he can be said to be partly responsible for the murder of one of them. Stavrogin's crime is not one of heroic action, but one of inaction in the awareness of catastrophe. He knows that having filled the world with his fragmented image, there is nothing he wishes to do to prevent total disintegration.

About the influence of evil, Leon Zander has made an inter-

esting observation, which can be well applied to *The Possessed*:
"In a whole series of characters Dostoevsky shows how the
evil principle, increasing in strength, expresses itself first by
automatism, then by becoming a man's 'double,' and finally
by completely splitting his personality so that the unity of the
human self is finally lost. . . . As soon as it becomes the domi-
nant force it immediately dissolves the human personality,
destroys its uniqueness and appears to man as something formless and featureless, rational and ironical, present in different
persons and different characters but always one and the
same."[41] In their proposal of such and similar statements, several critics agree that most of the characters around Stavrogin
are emanations of his evil spirit; they are his creation, his disci-
ples, his satellites.[42] Of the women around him each reflects a
part of his character.[43] There is Liza, his emotional double;
there is the wife of Shatov, his licentious counterpart; there is
Marya, the forsaken and crippled "Mother Russia"; and last,
there is Dasha, the unrecognized sacrificial spirit, always present, never submitted to. All four Stavrogin deserts: the first
three in life, the fourth in death. The men who live within his
sphere are many, and each partakes of a fragment of Stavrogin's
disaggregated personality. Pyotr represents the nihilistic revolutionary, Kirillov the self-deified man, Shatov the inarticulate
and murdered fatherland, Stepan the Old Order, Lebyadkin
the drunken libertine, and Fedka the devil. When the novel has
drawn to its conclusion, only Pyotr has survived the holocaust
as the sole noncommitted character: he remains to continue the
destruction of life.

The inexhaustible "evil principle" in Stavrogin finds its
counterpart in his "extraordinary physical strength," both in
his prowess and in his social relations with other figures. In this
respect he typifies the strength and cunning associated with
powers of satanic magnitude. Although he appears "listless,
quiet, rather morose," he is constantly on the alert. Being fated
to bring to a close the reign of uncertain disbelief, Stavrogin's
disintegration spreads its formless presence to fill other characters. His relation to Pyotr illustrates his malignant influence.
Stavrogin is the pretender to the throne of chaos, a throne
which Pyotr tries to help secure. The revolutionary figure is the

self-appointed leader of the Terrorists, is concerned more with political action than with belief.[44] His idea is to have Stavrogin initiate the political upheaval by proclaiming him to be the legendary Ivan the Tsarevitch. Pyotr suggests the destruction of Russia so that "the earth will weep for its old gods." Then we will say that your savior is "in hiding." "The rumor will spread over the land, 'We've seen him, we've seen him. . . . You are beautiful and proud as a God. . . . You'll conquer them, you'll have only to look, and you will conquer them. He is "in hiding" and will come forth bringing a new truth. . . . And the whole land will resound with the cry, "A new just law is to come" ' " (II, viii, 429–430). Stavrogin thinks all this madness, but he leaves Pyotr "without answering." Similarly, when Pyotr offers to do away with Marya and to bring him Liza for amusement, Stavrogin refuses to take his "ape" seriously and remains silent. Pyotr may be but a " 'démon mesquin' sec et cynique";[45] yet he is the relentless agent of chaos: he directs the violence released in the world by the lassitude of an unconcerned Stavrogin. His goals are tangible ones. He plots to cripple, "to level mountains," to establish "the right to dishonor," and to initiate a new system of "monstrous, disgusting vice which turns man into an abject, cowardly, cruel, and self-ish wretch." Stavrogin represents the death of moral and spiritual values; and Pyotr who claims to need him ("Without you I am nothing. Without you I am a fly, a bottled idea: Columbus without America" [II, viii, 426–427]), this Pyotr whom Stavrogin brings to life is the murderer of creation.

Unlike Pyotr, who continues to draw inspiration from Stavrogin after they are reunited in the country town, the other characters in the narrator's account withdraw from the creator of their ideas when they rightly interpret his silence as a disintegration into indifference. Once Stavrogin's followers were looking for a god, but the search was regarded as hopeless by the man they trusted to lead them so that in agony they now question the principles by which they were instructed to live. His associations with Kirillov and Shatov reflect Stavrogin's attitude. At the same time that he was indoctrinating Shatov with religious nationalism, Stavrogin had implanted in Kirillov a god-defying arrogance. Kirillov wants to kill God and become a godhead himself. "God is the pain of the fear of death. He who will conquer pain and terror will become himself a god"; yet, Kirillov admits, "God has tormented me all my life," and to stop the agony is to replace him (I, iii, 114–115). These ideas Kirillov has well remembered, and when Stavrogin comes to visit him he needs to revaluate them. Kirillov expounds his ideas, but after Stavrogin has muttered with disdain that these are "the old commonplaces of philosophy," he becomes aware of his master's insincerity. In reproach he acknowledges his dependence: "Remember what you have meant in my life, Stavrogin" (II, i, 238–242).

In the character of Kirillov Dostoevsky studies man's rebellion against his Creator.[46] His conclusion is that, having freed himself from belief in God, man is bound to deify himself: for if God does not exist, then man is Lord of the creation. As soon as man declares that everything is lawful, he becomes a helpless victim of his own passions, fears, and doubts. He finds himself in the trap of his impotence and corruption until the only act left to his freedom is suicide. Although Kirillov believes in the "eternal moments" of *this* life, he is willing to sacrifice himself, like Christ, to bring man immortality. But his death is not a Christian one—unless one considers his prompter to be like Judas whom Christ willed to force the moment to its crisis—because Kirillov fulfills his own will. As Berdyaev concludes: Kirillov ends "in a death that knows no resurrection; death is victorious over deified man."[47]

Stavrogin's next confrontation is with Shatov, the man who believes in the "god-bearing people" of Russia and who wants to but cannot believe in God, because, defined as "the synthetic personality of the whole people," He is but a nihilistic half-truth. Stavrogin has come to warn Shatov that his life is in danger, and that the revolutionaries plan to murder him as an informer. But Shatov, in perplexity over Stavrogin's complicity in the plot, cries out in disbelief that his "sun" to whom he is a mere "insect" in comparison should have wanted to join. Stavrogin replies that it was "by accident, as a man of leisure." Drop your detached air, Shatov insists, "Speak if only for once in your life with the voice of a man." Stavrogin continues to refute the present validity of his youthful utterances, and at last admits: "I wasn't joking with you then; in persuading you I was perhaps more concerned with myself than you." Furthermore, he remarks that "everyone of you for some inexplicable reason keeps foisting a flag upon me." This is precisely what Stavrogin does not want. If he were to assume bold leadership, he would risk having his fallibility exposed. Stavrogin prefers to remain within the system he has created. He has lost touch with the people, as Shatov suspects, by raising himself above humanity. Still, his stature is undiminished: "Why am I condemned to believe in you through all enternity?"; it is Shatov's cry and inasmuch as he is the emissary of the Russian people it is theirs as well (II, ii, 242–260).

Stavrogin wills to forget the past in which he "persuaded" himself that man's "yearning" must be directed toward a union with God and His Creation; he wills to forget his marriage to Marya "for a drunken bet," his rape of Matryosha for relief of boredom, and his betrayal of all friendships. "I hated it as . . . part of me" ("At Tihon's," 714). Stavrogin longs to escape to pre-Christian days and to return to the light and purity that were Greece. Like Clamence traveling across the "wet" void of the Zuyder Zee, Stavrogin makes his journey through the "rainy" hell on the bridge linking two darkened shores.

Once Stavrogin was given a vision of Eden: Claude Lorraine's painting "Acis and Galatea," which he greatly admired, had become an "actual" scene within a dream. "European mankind remembers this place," he tells Father Tihon, "as its cradle, and the thought filled my soul with the love that is bred of kinship. Here was mankind's earthly paradise. . . . The most improbable of all visions, to which mankind throughout its existence has given its best energies, for which it has sacrificed everything . . . and without which nations will not desire to live, and without which they cannot even die" ("At Tihon's," 715). Stavrogin has accepted the fact that this vision is dead (ironically, Lorraine's threatening Cyclops on the mountain, about to kill Acis, does not appear in the revelation). It is not to be recreated, Dostoevsky implies, so long as Western man continues to perpetrate the sham of his civilization, which thrives on the negation of human values. The "love that is bred of kinship" Adam and Cain destroyed. Man can but hate and so descend into his own hell. Like Stavrogin, he is "to go downhill," "to reach an empty expanse," and thus to find himself, when waking up "from a profound reverie," alone "in the middle of one long, wet, floating bridge." Stavrogin's dream has turned into a nightmare in which a Tempter asks for protection: "Will you kindly allow me, sir, to share your umbrella?" When Stavrogin looks closely, he recognizes Fedka, "the convict." "I stand before you, sir, as before God, because I have heard so much about you." He pulls back from this man who has "dropped from the sky" to escape the suave voice that insists: "But do you know the way here? There are all sorts of turnings. . . . I could guide you; for this town is for all the world as though the devil carried it in his basket and dropped it in bits here and there" (II, ii, 281–282; ellipsis in original).

Stavrogin *does* know the way through the labyrinth of chaos. It is his domain. From the beginning to the end of Stavrogin's career his actions and thoughts lead the way in the direction of breakdown and death. In him the sense of aspiration began its descent in St. Petersburg. The "bright falcon" who soared, "gazing at the sun," fell form the sky into the "pale blue" house where Matryosha lived. Marya recognizes the deception behind Stavrogin's mask, and she rejects his suggestion to follow him in a "forty years'" exile to the "gloomy" valley of Uri. "No, it cannot be that a falcon has become an owl. My prince is not like that." Despite the disillusion there is pride and triumph in her exclamation. As a spirit of the Russian earth she fully rejects the fallen valor of the false bearer of salvation.

Dostoevsky showed in Stavrogin's character a complete lack of positive development: he loves nothing; he doubts everything. In his *Notebook* Dostoevsky planned to have Stavrogin remark: "I consider myself . . . an independent unity and I shall say that others have betrayed me, not that I myself have betrayed others. Leave me. I stand alone. I am an egoist and I want to live within my egoism."[48] Because of this kind of negation, which Stavrogin must represent, he can travel in only one direction, out of a loveless past into a lifeless chaos, attesting to the total denial of the Promised Land. His very existence is what Camus called a horizontal one, inasmuch as he refuses to acknowledge what is beyond his world. It is an existence filled with his own Image from which he cannot escape through communion with others; he can merely appear as an aspect of self, incarnated in a Fedka or in a Kirillov. He signifies death-in-life and the reality of nothingness from the viewpoint of the world beyond his image; it is this "reality" to which mankind clings in its eagerness to find a firm footing, any footing in a nondefined world. Perpetually falling, Stavrogin is unable to find a place of rest. Trapped in his "cage" he is constantly shifting to find stability. He travels in the Orient; he goes to Mount Athos and stands through night services; he visits Egypt and Switzerland and sails as far as Iceland. And yet for the traveler there is no rest or fulfillment; absent-mindedly he passes the station where he ought to change for his destination. Whether at home or abroad, Stavrogin is well aware that he ruins the world and that not all the power in the universe can save him from his demonism. "Nothing comes to an end in this world" (II, iii, 297). But it does: he "was hanging there behind the door. On the table lay a piece of paper with the words in pencil: 'No one is to blame, I did it myself' " (III, viii, 688). To the narrator this scene proves premeditation and consciousness "up to the last moment." Stavrogin has destroyed the creator of his own universe, himself. He has escaped from his "malconfort," but his subversive influence will continue to spread in the Pyotrs who, in turn, become "everything" to *their* followers.

5

Melville's
Moby-Dick

IT WOULD BE INTERESTING TO SPECULATE WHAT MIGHT
have happened if Dostoevsky and Herman Melville had been
familiar with each other's work, but, as the case stands now,
this would be mere surmisal. The Russian writer does not
mention the American in his letters or notebooks. This is not
surprising if one considers that the only nineteenth-century
non-English attempts to publicize Melville came at a time when
Dostoevsky was starting his career as writer and only a few
years before his deportation to Siberia.[1] Dostoevsky had been
dead some decades when Melville interest reached Russia in
the wake of the Anglo-American revival of the 1920s.[2] Revers-
ing this matter of literary influence, we must also assume that
Melville did not discover Dostoevsky. His extant letters do not
refer to the Russian author, and, moreover, Merton Sealts'
extensive study of Melville's *Belesenheit* (reading) does not
list Dostoevsky.[3] These facts are hardly contrary to expecta-
tion, since Melville, in all likelihood, read no Russian and,
obviously, did not live to see Dostoevsky's works translated
into English.

The nineteenth century was not as congenial to a rapid dis-
semination of ideas as ours is, and so it is for authors of this
century to select and mix comparable ideas which arose inde-

pendently. A good case in point is Camus, who not only read
and adapted Dostoevsky, but who also familiarized himself
with the work of Melville. Camus mentions the American author in his notebooks[4] and suggests in his *Myth of Sisyphus*
that *Moby-Dick* (1851) is an example of "truly absurd" works.[5]
Some ten years after he had made this suggestion, he wrote an
appreciation of Melville in which the appeal the American author had for him becomes clear. Ahab's story can be read,
Camus suggests, as the fatal passion of the individual mad with
sorrow and loneliness, while the reader should remember that
it is a battle against evil. It is also an illustration of "the irre-
sistible logic that results in setting a just man up against Creation and the Creator, then against his fellow-man, and next himself."[6] From the date of this commentary it appears that Camus
had Melville in mind while he was preparing *The Fall*. Clamence, who poses as a leader of men, resembles the captain of
the *Pequod*. They both embark on a voyage to destroy the
"white" indifference which has maimed them and, in their
private obsession, they lead their crew to destruction. That a
strong, overall affinity existed, Leon S. Roudiez has noted in
his outstanding essay on Camus and *Moby-Dick*. Roudiez
draws parallels between the characters of Ahab and Caligula,
between the authors' shared preoccupation with the theme of
death, and further suggests "the analogy with Sisyphus' rock
of the unending putting out to sea and returning to port of
ships and sailors." But, in spite of similarities, Roudiez empha-
sizes that *Moby-Dick* "is not a major source in the usual literary
meaning of the term."[7]

Of course it is not necessary to apply the "term" rigorously
when it is observed that Melville's *Moby-Dick*, like Dostoevsky's *The Possessed*, may have suggested to Camus a dramatic
technique in constructing *The Fall*. Just as Dostoevsky's fondness for Schiller led him to use dramatic forms in *The Possessed*,
so Melville's fondness for Shakepeare may have resulted in
the use of the dramatic form in *Moby-Dick*.[8] In the review
"Hawthorne and His Mosses," Melville declares that Shakespeare's genius lies in "those occasional flashings-forth of the
intuitive Truth in him; those short, quick probings at the very
axis of reality,—these are the things that make Shakespeare,

Shakespeare. Through the mouths of the dark characters of Hamlet, Timon, Lear, and Iago, he craftily says, or sometimes insinuates the things which we feel to be so terrifically true."[9] Apparently, Melville felt that the method of presenting truth in the Shakespearean sense is dramatic portrayal of character —a fact which may have led him to consider an overall dramatic approach.

Several critics have divided *Moby-Dick* into a five-act drama and have concurred with Charles Olson's early suggestion that the book "has a rise and fall like the movement of an Elizabethan tragedy."[10] However, beyond this initial premise most similarities between critical opinions end. Olson's division was refuted by Newton Arvin, who holds that *Moby-Dick* most resembles an "epic," not a drama. Nevertheless, Arvin, speaking of "movements," does his own dividing of the novel,[11] as do several other critics.[12] Whichever way the novel is sectioned, it seems apparent that the Prologue, in which the major characters are introduced and the scene is set, ends with the second appearance of Elijah and that Act I begins with the sailing of the *Pequod* (XXII). In this act the remaining characters are introduced and the relationship between Ahab and his crew established. To propose a further division, Act II opens with "The Quarter-Deck" (XXXVI). There Ahab gathers his sailors and with his promise of reward for the catch of Moby Dick, the tension begins to rise. Act III begins with the introduction of the mystery that is Fedallah (L) and continues the mounting action (through the calm of chapters on cetology) to end in "The Doubloon" (XCIX) where in a climactic gathering the gold coin is admired as reward, and where the doom of each admirer is sealed. After the climax, the falling action of Act IV is concerned with Ahab's monomaniac vision and preparation until a catastrophe is reached and the *Pequod* is destroyed by Moby Dick. Ishmael's "Epilogue" ends the five-act dramatic structure of Melville's novel.

Not only can *Moby-Dick* be considered to be a sequence of acts, but several individual chapters are an act unto themselves. The dramatis personae of these chapters—Ahab, Starbuck, Stubb, Flask, Pip, and the carpenter—are presented in narrative chapters without a word of dialogue before they are presented in stage-set chapters. Ahab has the chapter where his first appearance on deck is described (XXVIII). In "Knights and Squires" (XXVI, XXVII) Starbuck, Stubb, Flask, and Pip have theirs; and the carpenter, like Ahab, deserves one all to himself (CVII). After these introductions, their soliloquies and dialogues begin. While these are introduced or being spoken, Ishmael, as narrator, is completely absent. Moreover, he is not explicitly present in the already mentioned quarter-deck scene, nor in the choric revelry of the world's sailors (XL), nor in the climactic corpusant scene (CXIX). Charles Feidelson, equating the "dramatic presentation" and "Ishmael's vision," suggests that "in the visionary status of the entire action," apparently "both Melville and Ishmael lose themselves."[13]

It seems only right that Ishmael should lose himself. After all, he is, as narrator, but a one-dimensional character in the finished novel—and this in spite of what Melville may have intended. Many are the roles Ishmael has been assigned by the critics, but what in essence many of the terms suggest is that Ishmael is a nonentity in Melville's fictional world. He is called Melville's "mask,"[14] he is referred to as "an abstraction from the full richness of American experience"[15] and "the delegated vision of Melville";[16] he is "nebulous and neutral"[17] and the contrast to Ahab's audacity and monomania.[18] And last, not least, he is "an exile" in a "world of moral tyranny."[19] Some interesting suggestions have been made by a few critics who have developed a theory of a multiple-faceted Ishmael. A workable suggestion seems to be Paul Brodtkorb's which holds that "Ishmael forces the reader back upon his own resources and prevents any direct relationship. . . . The reader is then forced to be and to project what is in himself."[20] This statement had been anticipated by Maurice Friedman who wrote that "The changing, ever-shifting point of view in *Moby-Dick* is representative of the ever-changing, ever-shifting attitude of man toward the reality that confronts him."[21] What these critics suggest is that Ishmael is Everyman: His is the "empty spot" provided by Melville into which the reader can move by becoming part of the dramatis personae who confront Ahab.

Ishmael is the average man, and as such he functions as the "chorus." He is caught up in the pale reflection of a violent

"beyond" that remains inscrutable. To approximate this tragedy, which is not within human comprehension, Melville chose
a loose adaptation of classical tragedy.[22] Several are the chapters which deal with whaling and its history—it appears that
these perform a two-fold function. First, they suggest *that*
part of the universe which Ishmael can comprehend; they are
his and the reader's probable reality. Second, they create a
lull in the violent action propelled by Ahab, so that the dramatic
tension is eased. In the chapters which deal with Ahab's tragedy, a formal and classical definition can be applied. Ahab *is*
king in his own realm and isolated from the people in his pride
and madness. His flaw is a hubris that dares to challenge the
very nature of the universe. His pursuit of the White Whale,
his proud, destructive passion, provides a "single" action; and
his inevitable destruction leaves the reader with a sense of pity
for a man who should have known better and a feeling of fear
that on another voyage in an indifferent universe there will be
no coffin to buoy him. The journey on the *Pequod*, which has
led Ahab from his desire for revenge to his self-annihilation,
takes place in a timeless world. It is a protracted instant in
time and as such provides a unity of duration. *Moby-Dick*
opens with a prologue; but once the *Pequod* sails, all action is
confined to the ship and the water surrounding it, and so is
presented a distinct unity of place.

Melville depicted a suitable stage for his tragic action. The
ship of mankind he called the *Pequod*, reminding the reader
that it is "the name of a celebrated tribe of Massachusetts
Indians, now extinct as the ancient Medes" (XVI, 68).[23] (The
name itself means "destroyer" in Algonquian Indian,[24] and,
according to the Puritans, it was associated with Satan.)[25] On
this "cannibal of a craft," with bulwarks "garnished like one
continuous jaw," Ahab rules the decks which are like the flag-
stones "where Becket bled" (XVI, 68–69). Within this realm
Ahab dominates the lonely height of the quarter-deck. He is
looked up to by all his crew but feared by those who understand his motives. Like Stavrogin, he draws his fictional audience as well as the reader into his monomaniacal world of wrath
and destruction; he lures all with promise of reward onto the
stage where, like Becket, they shall be killed for having dared
to challenge an existing order.

At the time Melville was writing *Moby-Dick*, he was much concerned with "the apprehension of the absolute condition of present things as they strike the eye of the man who fears them not." In a letter to Hawthorne in April 1851, he wrote of man's right to his own sovereignty in a world which may well be indifferent to his thoughts and actions. The man who takes this right, as Ahab did, "declares himself a sovereign nature (in himself) amid the powers of heaven, hell, and earth. He may perish; but so long as he exists he insists upon treating with all Powers upon an equal basis. If any of those other Powers choose to withhold certain secrets, let them; that does not impair my sovereignty in myself; that does not make me tributary. And perhaps, after all, there is *no* secret."[26] If this is so and if the mystery of Creation is discovered to be nonexistent, any enigma can take its place to provide the disappointed faithful with a surrogate Power. "Take God out of the dictionary," Melville concludes in the same letter, "and you would have him in the street." This is precisely what he set out to do in *Moby-Dick* when he sent Ahab on his journey to mislead the people.

As has been the case with Stavrogin, little is known of Ahab prior to his first appearance on the deck of the *Pequod*. It is stated that he only has one leg and that the other "was devoured, chewed up, crunched by the monstrousest parmacetty that ever chipped a boat." He is described as "a grand, ungodly, godlike man," and, like his biblical namesake, "a crowned king." It is predicted that his "name would somehow prove prophetic" (XVI, 71–80), which, as the rumors go, has turned out to be true. Ahab killed someone in front of an altar, spat into a communion cup, and then lost his leg on the homeward voyage. He started out believing that sacred places and man-created rituals could be taken for granted, but he ended up discovering that the object of man's veneration, the source of beauty and happiness, has been an abominable lie. In this realization Ahab has encountered the absurd, and as the narrative opens he has decided to avenge himself on that which assaulted his blessed state of injudicious autonomy.

In a new awareness the parmacetty whale now becomes Ahab's means of confronting the purposelessness of the universe. The all-destroying whale enables Ahab to wrest identity from a nameless force and to assert significance in the face of indifference. Ahab can find himself and know himself in the pursuit of the whale. He becomes an alien when his normal desire for revenge upon the White Whale develops into a monomania, a "madness maddened" (XXXVII, 166), which allows nothing to interfere with the consummation of his titanic revenge. His madness grew out of a personal injury, and so it is a personal victory he is seeking, a triumph of the self. This arrogance, together with his position of command, can lead only to isolation. However, unaided he cannot succeed, and by beguiling those who think they are gathering oil for the lamps of the world, he forms his band of avengers. As the deliberate misleader, Ahab appears in false disguises, and the crew too readily believe in him. They are fascinated when Ahab emerges from the "sacred retreat of the cabin," looking "like a man cut away from the stake" and seemingly made "of solid bronze." He does not speak, but, like Stavrogin, he only has to appear: his presence is enough to enthrall those who watch him high on the deck. "There was an infinity of firmest fortitude, a determinate, unsurrendable wilfulness, in the fixed and fearless, forward dedication of the glance. Not a word he spoke. . . . Moody stricken Ahab stood before them with a crucifixion in his face; in all the nameless regal overbearing dignity of some mighty woe" (XXVIII, 119–122). To suggest this overbearing woe, Ahab is depicted in mighty terms. He is made to wear, like Charlemagne and Napoleon, the "Iron Crown of Lombardy" while "damned in the midst of Paradise" (XXXVII, 165). He is the captain who, "though nominally included in the census of Christendom, . . . was still an alien to it" (XXXIV, 150). Melville is fond of grandiose epithets, and his favorite words (*wild, moody, mystic, nameless, intense,* and *malicious*) suggest dark and enigmatic themes of elemental strife.[27]

"Branded" Ahab, as well as Cain, is dedicated to violence, and in his obstinacy he scornfully confronts the doom of his mortality. Unable to get even with a Source of Evil that may well be without design, Ahab attacks the tangible reality which he can hold responsible. As Ishmael explains: "The White Whale swam before him as the monomaniac incarnation of all those malicious agencies which some deep men feel eating in them. . . . That intangible malignity which has been from the beginning; to whose dominion even the modern Christians ascribe one-half of the worlds. . . . All the subtle demonisms of life and thought; all evil, to crazy Ahab, were visibly personified, and made practically assailable in Moby Dick" (XLI, 181). The narrator rightly anticipates what is to follow. Ahab has now become convinced of a true existence of demonism in the world. From here on he can only endeavor to step outside the limitations of man to destroy a permanent order in the universe. In his resolution he may be called Promethean in so far that he is going to defy the gods, but the comparison does not truly hold because Ahab worships fire as the *destructive* element and himself creates the very monster that will destroy his body.

Once Ahab has been introduced, it is difficult to find a specific prototype after which he may have been designed. He partakes of many, but is none. Ahab's vital strength tempts Ishmael to describe the enigma which is his captain; but his powers of observation fail and he is forced to conclude that "Ahab's larger, darker, deeper part remains unhinted" (XLI, 183). Ahab himself does not fare much better: he knows "that to mankind he did long dissemble; in some sort, did still. But that thing of his dissembling was only subject to his perceptibility, not to his will determinate" (XLI, 183). Ahab must remain unknown to his fictional world to carry out his demonic role. For the reader Melville purposely has portrayed only that aspect of his hero which defines him: a grand will to destruction; the remainder of the character he has only sketched in. To provide additional dimensions critics have attempted to fit him into one or another mold of archetypal heroes. Henry F. Pommer has a full-length study that deals with the concept of Milton's Satan as reflected in Ahab.[28] Daniel G. Hoffman finds Melville's hero "more properly a Faust" who "commands and enchants his followers" and who ends up "a Satan, a sorcerer, an Antichrist."[29] Henry A. Murray concurs with Hoffman when he calls Ahab a "Lucifer," a Christ "in reverse."[30] Rudolf Sühnel thinks of a nineteenth-century phenomenon when he declares: "Ahab has his origins in romantic satanism"[31]—an opinion Lawrance Thompson must have found congenial when he suggested Manfred as well as Prometheus.[32] Some critics, not relating Ahab to any specific model, see him as a "one-legged incarnation of Evil,"[33] a "mechanical man,"[34] and a "self-appointed messiah"[35] expressing "civilized man's colossal error."[36] Apparently, the critics on their voyage to the heart of Ahab have beheld their pet image in the sea of interpretation. In the opening chapter of *Moby-Dick* Melville has offered a multiple interpretation to his readers when he has Ishmael speculate on Narcissus, "who because he could not grasp the tormenting, mild image he saw in the fountain, plunged into it and was drowned. But that same image, we ourselves see in all rivers and oceans. It is the image of the ungraspable phantom of life; and this is the key to it all" (I, 3). Lewis Mumford had this passage in mind when, speaking of the "eternal Narcissus in man," he concluded that "Moby Dick is a labyrinth, and that labyrinth is the universe."[37]

This statement is hardly surprising when it is kept in mind that several of the characters in the novels of a mature Melville, pursuing the unknown, find themselves alone in a maze of unfamiliar worlds. Redburn, on his first voyage, is confronted with Jackson, an Ahab-like character, of whom it is said that he is "such a hideous looking mortal, that Satan himself would have run from him." He is the man with the "infernal"-looking eye of a "wolf" Redburn cannot escape, so that at last he finds himself "a sort of Ishmael in the ship, without a single friend or companion."[38] White Jacket suffers the same fate on the *Neversink*. His ship has a captain who disappears "behind the scenes, like the pasteboard ghost in Hamlet." He is unaware that his sailors have singled out the man with the white jacket as ghostly and "infernal," or that he arbitrarily has been refused paint—in a touch Kafka would have been proud of— "when but one dab of paint would make a man of a ghost."[39] The hero of *Mardi*, the man with the assumed name of Taji, starts his journey believing that there is "no soul a magnet to mine; none with whom to mingle sympathies." When the voyage to the land of Mardi is over, he exclaims: "Let me, then, be the unreturning wanderer." By proposing this, he is following the advice of the Mardian philosopher, Babbalanja, who realized that "up and down we wander, like exiles transported to a planet afar."[40] Melville seems to suggest here that we approach the summit of our experience utterly disinherited.

After *Moby-Dick* a changed Melville seems to have given up the hope that all man has to do is set out on the road of life to discover its meaning. The characters of the later novels become, willy-nilly, victims of a fatalistic universe. In his "Introduction" to *Pierre or the Ambiguities*, Henry Murray makes the following observation: "Melville's position in *Mardi* might be defined in these words: 'If I fail to reach my golden haven, may my annihilation be complete!'; in *Moby-Dick*: 'I see that I am to be annihilated, but against this verdict I shall hurl an everlasting protest!'; in *Pierre*: 'I must make up my mind, if possible, to the inevitability of my annihilation; . . . and in 1891, in *Billy Budd*: 'I accept my annihilation.' "[41] With *Pierre* the serpent has entered Melville's fictional world. His hero of the Ambiguities lives in the Eden of his family estate until one day the sin of his father is visited upon him. Entering a self-imposed penance, he discovers "that the uttermost ideal of moral perfection in man is wide of the mark. The demi-gods trample on trash, and Vice and Virtue are trash!"[42] And in Melville's literary testament, Billy Budd, "practically a fatalist," is made to taste "the questionable apple of knowledge" when tempted to murder by "alien eyes" of "serpent fascination."[43]

Within a serpent-controlled world, as the Eden myth has suggested, isolation is man's natural state. In this condition the Abels may be destroyed, while the Cains, having tasted God's injustice, must flee into a purposeless universe. In order to survive they set up their own autonomous realm in which their reign over the blessedly ignorant can rival God's.

Isolation is also a significant theme in *Moby-Dick*. It is introduced in the first pages of Ishmael's reflections on the "insular city of the Manhattoes" where "silent sentinels all around the town" stand "in ocean reveries" (I, 1). As an underlying theme it is repeated in the chapter before Ahab's first appearance: "They were nearly all Islanders in the Pequod, *Isolatoes* too, I call such, . . . each Isolato living on a separate continent of his own. Yet now, federated along one keel" (XXVII, 118). They are awaiting the coming of the man who they hope will unite them in one common purpose. Whereas Ishmael is left at the end to tell that there was no continent of brotherhood, the others perish with their false leader.

Ahab himself lives in self-imposed exile. He only emerges
after several days of seclusion in his cabin. When he appears on
deck, he speaks no word; and even at dinner with his mates
Ahab rules his ivory kingdom[44] "like a mute, maned sea-lion
on the white coral beach, surrounded by his warlike but still
deferential cubs" (XXXIV, 147). The scene symbolizes the distance which exists between Ahab and those who should be
closest to him. Ahab is himself fully aware of his solitary state.
In two of the very few instances in the narrative in which he
speaks of the loneliness of his demonic mission, he admits to
Starbuck: "When I think of this life I have led; the desolation
of solitude it has been; the masoned, walled-town of a Captain's
exclusiveness, which admits but small entrance to any sympathy from the green country without—oh! weariness! heavi-
ness! Guinea-coast slavery of solitary command." But Ahab
knows that he is "branded" and is aware that, having dragged
"the judge to the bar," he must bring about his own doom
(CXXXIII, 534–536). "Begone," he tells his mates on the first
day of the chase, "ye two are all mankind; and Ahab stands
alone among the millions of the peopled earth, nor gods, nor
men his neighbors" (CXXXIV, 545). Therefore Ahab has but
one thing left to do when confronted with the havoc in which
he has been instrumental. Knowing that in the end the whale
cannot be conquered, he chooses his own destruction, since he
can work his vengeance on himself alone. He must lay down
his life, not *for* others, but *with* all the others he has caught in
his web of conspiracy.

Like Stavrogin, Dostoevsky's great sinner, Ahab gains diabolical control over the souls of his followers; by spreading evil,
he turns them into men possessed. In the impressive "Quarter-
Deck" chapter, Ahab emerges from his cabin with "ever-pacing
thought" and orders Starbuck to send everybody aft. Looking
at the apprehensive faces, Ahab pits his determined will against
the assembled power of the men. The nailing of the reward
doubloon, the proclamation that it was the White Whale "some
call Moby Dick" that "dismasted" their captain, the joining of
hands to signify the common bond of revenge, and the grog
drinking seal the brotherhood of annihilation which Ahab has
conceived. The diabolical ritual ends with a draught "hot as

Satan's hoof." Ahab looks at his band of conspirators and can feel satisfied as their eyes meet his, "as the bloodshot eyes of the prairie wolves meet the eye of their leader, ere he rushes on at their head in the trail of the bison; but alas! only to fall into the hidden snare of the Indian."

Only one person on board has realized the madness of being enraged by a dumb animal. Starbuck requires "a little lower layer" which Ahab willingly provides: "All visible objects, man, are but as pasteboard masks. But in each event—in the living act, the undoubted deed—there, some unknown but still reasoning thing puts forth the mouldings of its feature from behind the unreasoning mask! If man will strike, strike through the mask! How can the prisoner reach outside except by thrusting through the wall? To me, the white whale is that wall, shoved near to me. Sometimes I think there's naught beyond. . . . . I'd strike the sun if it insulted me" (XXXVI, 157–165). Starbuck retreats in horror, having glimpsed the depth of Ahab's nihilism. Having retreated to the mainmast, he cries out in anguish: "My soul is more than matched; she's over-manned; and by a madman. . . . Who's over him, he cries;— aye, he would be a democrat to all above; look, how he lords it over all below! Oh! I plainly see my miserable office,—to obey, rebelling; and worse yet, to hate with touch of pity" (XXXVIII, 166–167). Starbuck has a sense of decency and common humanity which he shares with Dostoevsky's Shatov. Both represent the native soil their leaders forsake and destroy in order to rise to godly heights. Pity has no place in a universe that lacks positive purpose and Ahab, trying to discover if there is anything hidden behind the visible Creation, must shatter the wall to be free. Starbuck's human compassion is an obstacle and as such must be eliminated.

Before the *Pequod* voyage, Starbuck had known of the White Whale only through common talk, and to him that whale always remained a dangerous opponent for which one risks one's life in the whaling business. He knows of people killed in the whale hunt, but he considers this a professional hazard. He kills whales for a living, not for a thrill, or not for that matter for any "heaven-insulting purpose" (XXXVIII, 167). He is what Chase has called "the only *homme moyen sensuel*" in the novel. "His

name indicates this," Chase explains; "it is a common one in
Nantucket; and the other characters all have biblical, barbaric,
or comic names."[45] He is a human being with instinctive love
for his land, his home, and his family. He does not consider
the killing of the whale a bid for glory, because he is no
"crusader after perils" (XXVI, 113). Content to trust in God
and to hunt whales for a living, he is, in John Bernstein's words,
"the only man of true Christian faith in the novel. When Starbuck speaks, the voice of Christianity is heard."[46]

To Stubb, Ahab's second mate, sailing and hunting are won-
derful sports, and conscience is a "toothache" the Lord inflicts.
"Think not, is my eleventh commandment" (XXIX, 125), he
says, because "a laugh's the wisest, easiest answer to all that's
queer." Stubb never thinks about God, but he has his own
comfort in the belief that "it's all predestinated" (XXXIX, 168).
In spite of his enthusiasm for whaling, Ahab does not like him
because he does not think. Stubb tries to cheer up Ahab after
he has been nearly drowned in the first assault on Moby Dick
and calls his captain's wrecked boat "the thistle the ass refused." Ahab snarls back: "Did I not know thee brave as fearless fire (and as mechanical) I could swear thou wert a poltroon"
(CXXXIII, 545). Stubb damns the devil and derides God, "the
old governor," who signed a bond "that all the people the devil
kidnapped, he'd roast for him" (LXXIII, 325). In short, Stubb
is indifferent to spiritual and intellectual affairs, and, to him,
the killing of Moby Dick is but another challenge.

Ishmael looks at the duo and concludes that Ahab cannot
expect much help from "the incompetence of mere unaided
virtue or right-mindedness in Starbuck, the invulnerable jollity
of indifference and recklessness in Stubb" (XLI, 184). Starbuck
is the only one who goes to his doom with open eyes. He has, as
Ishmael hinted, realized "the fall of valor in the soul" (XXVI,
113). Until the last day before Moby Dick is sighted, Starbuck
has kept hope that Ahab may yet be dissuaded. On this "clear
steel-blue day" he approaches Ahab under the protection of
"snow-white wings of small, unspeckled birds" that glide
above. In this scene, which strangely anticipates the doves over
Clamence's Amsterdam, Ahab rejects his last chance for redemption through faith and leaves Starbuck, "blanched to a

corpse's hue with despair" (CXXXII, 536), to join Fedallah, his private harpooner.

This Fedallah has been as much an enigma to Ahab's crew as he has been to the readers of *Moby-Dick*. William Braswell dismisses the matter by saying that he is "obviously a sort of Mephistopheles to Ahab."[47] Dorothee Grdseloff explains his role by analyzing the Arabian meaning of his name ("the Sacrifice or Ransom of God").[48] Arvin sees him in general terms as "a principle of pure negation,"[49] while others, perhaps closer to the mark, see him as Ahab's Double. Of this group the more explicit statement is M. O. Percival's which maintains that Fedallah "is not really an external agent, sent to tempt a certain victim by arrangement with the Lord; he is the creation of Ahab's own self-seducing mind."[50] Ahab himself brought Fedallah on board and, as himself, hid him for several days. The first time the boats are lowered, the seeming phantom suddenly appears. Fedallah, or the Parsee, as he is also called, is "swart" and dressed in black. His shadowy companions are natives of the Manillas, "a race notorious for a certain diabolism of subtilty, and by some honest white mariners supposed to be the paid spies and secret confidential agents on the water of the devil" (XLVIII, 215). Melville, like Dostoevsky, never calls his fictional apparitions devils, but, instead, has his diseased or superstitious characters make that observation. As Stubb declares: "I take that Fedallah to be a devil in disguise." He is a presence aboard for one purpose only. "Do ye see," Stubb says, "the old man is hard bent after that White Whale, and the devil there is trying to come round him, and get him to swap . . . his soul, . . . and then he'll surrender Moby Dick" (LXXIII, 324).

Most of the time, though, Fedallah is made to appear an extension of Ahab: "Ahab chanced so to stand, that the Parsee occupied his shadow; while, if the Parsee's shadow was there at all it seemed only to blend with, and lengthen Ahab's" (LXXIII, 327). Once, when Ahab is anxiously awaiting the first sign of Moby Dick, his "despot" eye watches Fedallah, who has grown thin and eerie like "a tremulous shadow cast upon the deck by some unseen being's body" (CXXX, 527). In the final scene before the chase begins, Ahab, gazing at the water, "started at two reflected, fixed eyes in the water there. Fedallah

was motionlessly leaning over the same rail" (CXXXII, 536).
And so they exist together "fixedly gazing upon each other;
as if in the Parsee Ahab saw his forethrown shadow, in Ahab
the Parsee his abandoned substance" (CXXX, 528).

Ahab's unholy alliance is also emphasized in other scenes.
When he welds his own harpoon with which to kill the White
Whale, he demands blood, the "true death-temper," from his
harpooneers to cool the steel. " 'Ego non baptizo te in nomine
patris, sed in nomine diaboli!' deliriously howled Ahab, as the
malignant iron scorchingly devoured the baptismal blood"
(CXIII, 484). One night the "corpusants" appear: "each of the
three tall masts" is "silently burning in that sulphurous air."
Stubb curses, failing to see that God has written a burning
"Mene, Mene, Tekel Upharsin" across the ship. Ahab, deliriously, puts his foot upon Fedallah and grabs the mainmast
links to feel the fire's "pulse" against his own. Ahab prays to
the light that is leaping out of darkness, and suddenly a
mysterious and pale flame appears at the tip of Ahab's very
own harpoon. He waves it among the crew and then, in a final
gesture of defiance, he extinguishes the flame with one blast of
his breath. Ahab blows out the light which has lit up the darkness (CXIX 498–502).[51] He has now been shown the way to
the White Whale.

Ever since his first encounter with Moby Dick, Ahab has
hated him, be he "principal" or "agent." He has piled upon his
white hump the rage of mankind, but whether Moby Dick is a
divinity, Evil personified, or only a manifestation of a malignly
indifferent universe, Ahab has never decided. It is enough to
believe in the hate for that "inscrutable thing" (XXXVI, 162).
It is impossible to comprehend this whale to which many critics
attribute divine power or divine essence. Arvin's comments are
representative of what most critics have observed. He sees
Moby Dick, not as a Calvinistic God, but as "a grandiose
mythic presentation of what is godlike in the cosmos," as an
animal deity of "always overbearing and unconquerable
force."[52] Moby Dick, then, is beauty and wisdom, and, as
energy, he is the unreasoning force of chaos, the destroyer of
rival power which seeks to know him. His incomprehensible
role as executioner of man shall remain unexplained, and all the

"superstitious" will ever know is that Moby Dick is "ubiqui-
tous" (XLI, 179).

One does not have to be an Ahab to realize that "the problem
of the universe" is revolving in him. Ishmael knows it too
(XXXV, 155). When Ahab unites his crew in unholy sacrament,
Ishmael, like the reader, experiences "a wild, mystical feeling"
(XLI, 175). As thoughtful narrator—and as Melville's spokesman—he ponders on the whiteness of the whale, a detail which
lies outside the dramatic development of the narrative and as
such is not given significance for Ahab. The captain is primarily
aware of the physical entity of the whale, and it is for Ishmael
to suggest that "the supernaturalism of the hue" should remind
the fairy tale reader of the headless horseman of the Hartz
forest (XLII, 189–191). Whiteness is formlessness, an in-
definite blank, and beauty and meaning are "but subtile deceits,
not actually inherent in substances, but only laid on from without" by the observer. "All deified Nature absolutely paints like
the harlot, whose allurements cover nothing but the charnel-
house within. . . . Pondering all this, the palsied universe lies
before us a leper" (XLII, 193–194).[53] It is this statement which a
less-speculative Ahab wants to verify. But in his pursuit even
Ahab, when his "tormented spirit" disassociates itself from his
monomania, becomes a meaningless being. He is then "a
vacated thing, a formless somnambulistic being, a ray of living
light, to be sure, but without an object to color, and therefore
a blankness in itself" (XLIV, 200).

Of the *Pequod's* crew, Ahab is the only one in whom super-
natural worlds manifest themselves, and therefore he is also,
at times, the void of total estrangement. He alone is free to deny
his bonds with the cardboard security of tradition and happiness. Having risen above the blissful ignorance of mankind, he
can, like Meursault, extend a gratuitous gesture of kindness
and allow a harmless idiot the use of his cabin. Ahab does not
need Starbuck's conscience or love or duty, since these are
qualities that bind man to man. "Science! Curse thee, thou vain
toy," he yells, and cursed are all things "that cast man's eye
aloft" to heaven (CXVIII, 494). Man's go-between for himself
and the universe Ahab rejects as intolerable deceiver of harmonious existence. In one of the more climactic scenes toward

the conclusion of the novel, Ahab rejects the last plea mankind brings to him: to help search for the lost son of the captain of the *Rachel*. "I will not do it," he tells the begging father, "God bless ye, man, and may I forgive myself, but I must go" (CXXVIII, 524). Ahab cannot rest until he has eliminated the only force which prevents him from being absolute ruler in his autonomous realm.

Ahab's determination is nowhere more evident than in his reaction to the encounter with other worlds that have not come under his demonic influence. These encounters take the form of the *Pequod's* nine "gams," the social meetings of Ahab's ship with other whalers (LIII, 239).[54] Ahab's estrangement and his singleness of purpose stand out in the face of this natural and customary sociability, since he will not "consort, even for five minutes, with any stranger captain, except he could contribute some of that information he so absorbingly sought" (LIII, 236). When the *Pequod* meets another ship, Ahab's one question is, "Have ye seen the White Whale?" The captain of the *Enderby* has not only seen the White Whale, but has lost his arm as a result of him. "There would be great glory in killing him, . . . but, hark ye, he's best let alone." But to Ahab it is just this fact which has given purpose to his life. "He is," Ahab admits, "but he will still be hunted, for all that. What is best let alone, that accursed thing is not always what least allures. He is all a magnet" (C, 439). The *Enderby* at least has encountered Moby Dick, but the jolly *Bachelor*, like Stubb, cannot even take him seriously. Its captain stands erect on his quarter-deck, enjoying his ship of "jubilation." Ahab, in contrast, stands on the deck of the "moody *Pequod*," "shaggy and black, with a stubborn gloom" (CXV, 488–489).

Perhaps the most distinct indication of Ahab's monomaniac life is the doubloon which he nails to the mast as a prize for the first man who sights Moby Dick. When, one after the other, Ahab and some crew members read the design on the doubloon, the coin "to each and every man in turn, but mirrors back his own mysterious self," as Ahab knows. And only Ahab sees it as himself: "There's something ever egotistical in mountain-tops and towers, and all other grand and lofty things; look here,—three peaks as proud as Lucifer. The firm tower, that is

Ahab; the volcano, that is Ahab; the courageous, the un-
daunted, and victorious fowl, that, too, is Ahab; all are Ahab."
Each sees reality from his own perspective, as little Pip indicates in the last interpretation: "I look, you look, he looks; we
look, ye look, they look" (XCIX, 428–432). But only Ahab
identifies himself with mountaintops to the exclusion of all un-
lofty things. It is appropriate that it is Ahab himself who first
"raises" Moby Dick and then claims the doubloon for his own.
He does not fail to draw the proper conclusion from this hap-
pening. " 'I saw him almost that same instant, sir, that Captain
Ahab did, and I cried out,' said Tashtego. 'Not the same instant;
not the same—no, the doubloon is mine, Fate reserved the
doubloon for me. *I* only; none of ye could have raised the White
Whale first' " (CXXXIII, 538). Ahab reaps his own reward and
refuses to share his misleadership as destructive visionary.

Like Dostoevsky's heroes, Ahab dreams of paradise, but he
is brought low by the vision of evil which interposes itself. On
the third day of the chase his thoughts wander off to other
times: "Let me have one more good round look aloft here at
the sea; there's time for that. An old, old sight, and yet somehow so young; aye, and not changed a wink since I first saw it,
a boy, from the sandhills of Nantucket! The same!—the same!
—the same to Noah as to me. There's a soft shower to leeward.
Such lovely leewardings! They must lead somewhere—to something else than common land, more palmy than the palms. Leeward! the white whale goes that way; look to windward, then;
the better if the bitterer quarter" (CXXXV, 557). In his
moment of clarity Ahab realizes his loss and, driven by compulsion, he goes to his doom like Raskolnikov, Kirillov, Stavrogin, and Ivan Karamazov. Worldly order and divinely promised harmony are hateful concepts to Ahab because they limit
his personal freedom. He must confront them and refuse to
compromise. To adandon the chase of the White Whale is to be
less than a conqueror: Ahab cannot relent. "Oh, now I feel my
topmost greatness lies in my topmost grief. Ho, ho! from all
your furthest bounds, pour ye now in, ye bold billows of my
whole foregone life, and top this one piled comber of my death!
Towards thee I roll, thou all-destroying but unconquering
whale; to the last I grapple with thee; from hell's heart I stab

at thee; for hate's sake I spit my last breath at thee" (CXXXV,
565). With passionate defiance Ahab rages on, undefeated in
his self-centered approbation. He has not given a thought to
the "unnecessary duplicates" (CVII, 462) he led to their death
for the gratification of his own ambition.

In this fatal pride he rails against divine injustice, while as-
suming that mankind will be served by his brand of nihilism.
He denies God, but forgets that this will only lead to the attempt to replace him. In his single-minded ascent Ahab has
only affirmed his own life and abandoned his illusions together
with his lost leg. Ahab knows, as do Camus' and Dostoevsky's
heroes, that life is only lived to the fullest in contention with
opposing forces. But the secret for happiness in this contest lies
in the recognition of each man's solidarity with mankind. The
neglect of this factor becomes the undoing of the New England
captain, as well as that of Stavrogin and Clamence. This flaw
in their zeal turns them into misleaders and destroyers of those
they bring under their influence.

Ahab's quest, in the last analysis, reduces to Melville's own
search for the answers to the eternal questions: What is the
nature of man's relation to the reality which surrounds him?
Why is man not allowed absolute knowledge so that he can
distinguish between appearance and reality? And how is he to
know the good that allows evil? The answers are implicit in
the words and deeds of Captain Ahab. "Ahab is for ever Ahab,
man. This whole act's immutably decreed. 'Twas rehearsed by
thee and me a billion years before this ocean rolled. Fool! I am
the Fates' lieutenant; I act under orders. Look thou, underling!
that thou obeyest mine.—Stand round me, men. . . . I feel
strained, half-stranded, as ropes that tow dismasted frigates in
a gale; and I may look so. But ere I break, ye'll hear me crack;
and till ye hear *that*, know that Ahab's hawser tows his purpose
yet" (CXXXIV, 554). Man's relation to the outside world is
what he believes it to be. Man's knowledge is relative because
he acts under orders of the unknown, the inexplicable, and the
irrational. Man is a prisoner so long as he is lamed by fear.
Ahab's anchor cable must tow him yet, until he has come face
to face with what he believes is the source of the absurdity of
existence. Man's life is like the labor of Sisyphus. Freedom and

insight are his only when he accepts pain and suffering without fear and without hope, when he succeeds in developing his love to encompass others, when he can unite in human reality. Only then will he be able to experience a human solidarity to counteract the indifference of a chaotic universe.

6

Conclusion

THE WORLD WHICH CAMUS, MALRAUX, KAFKA, Dostoevsky, and Melville have described is not "another" world visible through the veil of memory, beyond the lost horizon of yesterday's barely seen land, or behind the footlight of a play others have performed. It is the world of "I" and hopefully "We" which reveals a clarity of artistic vision that pertains to the present moment. For the main characters of the fictional world the "otherness" of existence had already taken place before they were introduced to the reader. Yet, the essence of the fictional characters, formed by "otherness," has moved along the ever-extending boundary of this and another world, never redeemed, never initiated into solidarity and action by a revelation of falseness or anarchy. The reader has been instructed by negative example. In their proposal of a counteraction for the salvation of man, Camus in *The Fall*, Dostoevsky in *The Possessed*, and Melville in *Moby-Dick* have cast statements of extreme pessimism intended as mirrors in which the reader could see the disastrous results of both selfish commitment and lack of involvement. These three novelists, and Malraux and Kafka as well, have found man to be a solitary creature without any orientation map in the labyrinth of this cardboard security, a creature led by prophetic characters from whom there issued commands to force the scattered disbelievers in Christian salvation to join in a parody of their humanity. Once these self-appointed leaders, these false prophets, had understood what they believed to have been the caprice of their earlier ideals, they took up the banner of absolute dictatorship. It is evident that they had known man's weakness and hunger for love, knowledge, and power, and, in this knowledge, had occupied an eminent position preserved by a promise of a common good. A free man is always faced with this question: Are there moral norms and limits in my nature which I must obey even if I do not follow the prescribed ways of a culture? For the fatally disappointed in humanity the answer is no. For them freedom is allowed to degenerate into a self-will that holds nothing as sacred or forbidden, because if there is no god or essence of self then everything is permitted and man can act at will. At the same time they let themselves become obsessed by some fixed idea and under its shadow they stave off their own collapse. In their experiments for survival they depend on the folly of believers who mistake tyranny for guidance. Eventually, these emissaries of limitlessness are destroyed in their lack of compassion; they think that in the name of collective disenchantment and equality for all, it is permitted to seduce other beings into a support of a hollow ideal: themselves. Their victims had lost their spiritual destiny once they had been deprived of their humanity. Never having discovered the bounds of human nature because of their failure to commune with their own, untried essence, they contracted away the spirit in exchange for any promising future security. Unable to have been their own keeper, they were to remain children of darkness confined in eagerly sought bounds that would protect them from an infinite unknown. Still unfulfilled and being lost in endless corridors of solitude, man turned inward toward an empty self from where his free spirit was bartered off to a convincing voice crying in the wilderness, to one which could lead him away from the abyss of eternal nothingness. Obsessed with the desire to be rescued at any cost, man eventually turns into an instrument manipulated by misleaders possessed by aggressive delusions to be inflicted upon others.

It has long been known that the West is not the best of all

possible worlds and that all is not well though God may be in heaven. Camus, Dostoevsky, and Melville have restated that. They feel that so long as Western man continues to perpetrate the sham of a cultural system which thrives upon the negation of human values, he cannot enjoy the love of kinship; in hate, he must descend into his own hell. He can travel in only one direction: out of a loveless past into a lifeless chaos, attesting to the total denial of the Promised Land. He does not see man in God's image, but he always encounters his self incarnated in others. The false prophets of the novelists signify life-in-death to those who believe, and the reality of nothingness to those outside this destructive sphere. Man's relation to the outside world is what he believes it to be. Man's knowledge is relative because he acts under orders of the unknown, the inexplicable, and the irrational. Man is a prisoner so long as he is maimed by fear. Man's life is indeed like the labor of Sisyphus. Freedom and insight are his only when he lives through pain and suffering without fear and without hope for the unattainable. He must unite to confront, in solidarity, the indifference of the universe.

Notes

A Literary Climate, 1860–1960

[1] L. F. Céline, *Journey to the End of Night,* tr. John H. P. Marks (London: Penguin Books, 1966), p. 367.

[2] Marcel Arland, "Sur un nouveau Mal du Siècle," *La Nouvelle Revue Française,* XXII (February 1924), 157.

[3] Friedrich Nietzsche, *The Joyful Wisdom,* tr. Thomas Common (London: T. N. Foulis, 1910), section 108, p. 151.

[4] Paul Tillich, "Protestantism and Artistic Style," in *The Theology of Culture* (New York: Oxford University Press, 1959), p. 70.

[5] Albert Camus, *Noces* (Paris: Editions Charlot, 1937), p. 93.

[6] Albert Camus, *Actuelles I; Chroniques 1944–1948* (Paris: Gallimard, 1950), p. 225.

[7] André Malraux, *The Temptation of the West,* tr. Robert Hollander (New York: Vintage Books, 1961), p. 118.

[8] Albert Camus, "Lettre au directeur des *Temps Modernes,"* *Les Temps Modernes,* VIII (August 1952), 320.

[9] André Malraux, "Réponse à Léon Trotsky," *La Nouvelle Revue Française,* XXXVI (April 1931), 502.

[10] André Malraux, *The Conquerors,* tr. Winifred S. Whale (Boston: Beacon Press, 1956), p. 164 (the translation has chosen "vanity" for Malraux' choice of "absurde").

[11] André Malraux, *The Royal Way,* tr. Stuart Gilbert (New York: Vintage Books, 1955), p. 142.

[12] Gustav R. Hocke in *Die Welt als Labyrinth* (Hamburg: Rowohlt, 1959), II, 90, 272, sees the world as a labyrinth in which man

searches for "Vereinigung des Disparaten" (union of disparities), but where, for lack of exit, he can do little else but destroy himself.

[13] Hannah Arendt in "Franz Kafka: A Revaluation," *Partisan Review*, XI (Fall, 1944), 412-422, holds that Kafka depicted society "as a substitute for God"; society rejects K. because of his normalcy. Erich Heller in *The Disinherited Mind* (London: Bowes and Bowes, 1957), pp. 199–231, sees the Castle as the realm of demons which haunt man.

[14] André Malraux, *Man's Hope*, tr. Stuart Gilbert and Alastair MacDonald (New York: Random House, 1938), p. 320.

[15] Paul Valéry, *Introduction to the Method of Leonardo da Vinci*, tr. T. McGreevy (London: John Rodker, 1929), p. 24. Man "passes nine-tenths of his time in what has yet to happen, in that which no longer is, in what cannot possibly be; to such an extent that our true *present* has nine chances out of ten of never being."

[16] For brief commentary on "*ex cathedra* reflections," see A. A. Mendilow, *Time and the Novel* (London: Peter Nevill, 1952), p. 110.

[17] André Malraux, *Man's Fate*, tr. Haakon M. Chevalier (New York: Modern Library, 1934), p. 159.

[18] Paul Valéry, "Autour de Corot" in *Pièces sur l'art* (Paris: Editions de la *NRF*, 1938), p. 151.

[19] Charles Baudelaire, *Art in Paris: 1845–1862; Salons and Other Exhibitions*, tr. and ed. J. Mayne (London: Phaidon Press, 1965), p. 47.

[20] Jacques Maritain, "Concerning Poetic Knowledge," in J. and R. Maritain, *The Situation of Poetry* (New York: Philosophical Library, 1955), pp. 44, 47.

[21] Murray Krieger, *The Tragic Vision* (Chicago: University of Chicago Press, 1960), pp. 1–21.

[22] Erich Kahler sees the parable as a possibly new modern genre, and he defines it as a story "on an abstract, rarefied level, lifted out of specific locale, time and individual characteristics—a story that pictures our human condition in an immediately supra-individual manner, without losing its human intensity and vividness." See his "The Transformation of Modern Fiction," *Comparative Literature*, VII (1955), 126–127.

[23] Rudolf Otto, *Das Heilige; über das Irrationale in der Idee des Göttlichen und sein Verhältnis zum Rationalen* (Breslau: Trewendt und Granier, 1917), Ch. V, pp. 26–32.

[24] Malraux, *The Royal Way*, p. 250.

[25] Mario Praz, *The Romantic Agony*, tr. Angus Davidson (New York: World Publishing, 1956), p. 438.

[26] *Ibid., passim.*

[27] J. A. Boiffard, P. Eluard, and R. Vitrac, editorial in *La Révolution Surréaliste*, No. 1 (December 1924), as reprinted in Patrick Waldberg, *Surrealism* (New York: McGraw-Hill, 1965), p. 48.

[28] Wallace Fowlie, *Age of Surrealism* (Bloomington: Indiana University Press, 1960), p. 24.

[29] Max Brod, *Franz Kafka; eine Biographie* (Berlin: S. Fischer Verlag, 1954), pp. 205–238, and his "Nachwort zur ersten Ausgabe," in Franz Kafka, *Das Schloss* (New York: Schocken Books, 1946), pp. 415–424. Albert Camus, "Hope and the Absurd in the Work of Franz Kafka," in *The Myth of Sisyphus and other Essays*, tr. Justin O'Brien (New York: Vintage Books, 1955), pp. 92–102. Norbert Fürst, *Die offenen Geheimtüren Franz Kafkas* (Heidelberg: Wolfgang Rothe Verlag, 1956), pp. 16–35. Felix Weltsch, *Religion und Humor im Leben und Werk Franz Kafkas* (Berlin: F. A. Herbig, 1957).

[30] See below, p. 92.

[31] René Girard, *Mensonge romantique et vérité romanesque* (Paris: B. Grasset, 1961), p. 65.

[32] Friedrich Nietzsche, *The Birth of Tragedy*, tr. W. A. Haussmann (London: T. N. Foulis, 1909), p. 68.

[33] Krieger, *The Tragic Vision*, p. 10.

[34] Richard B. Sewall, *The Vision of Tragedy* (New Haven: Yale University Press, 1959), p. 85. George Steiner, *Tolstoy or Dostoevsky* (New York: Vintage Books, 1961), pp. 135 ff.

[35] Northrop Frye, *Anatomy of Criticism* (Princeton: Princeton University Press, 1957), pp. 33–34.

[36] Sewall, *The Vision of Tragedy*, p. 110.

[37] Nietzsche, *The Birth of Tragedy*, p. 69.

[38] André Malraux, "Author's Preface" to *Days of Wrath*, tr. Haakon M. Chevalier (New York: Random House, 1936), p. 3.

[39] Joseph W. Beach, *The Twentieth Century Novel* (New York: Appleton-Century, 1932), pp. 148, 181.

[40] Frye, *Anatomy of Criticism*, p. 269.

[41] Mendilow, *Time and the Novel*, p. 112.

Camus' The Fall

[1] John Cruickshank, *Albert Camus and the Literature of Revolt* (New York: Oxford University Press, 1960), p. 183.

[2] Germaine Brée, *Camus* (Rev. ed.; New York: Harcourt, Brace and World, 1964), p. 133.

[3] Carl A. Viggiani, "Camus and the Fall from Innocence," *Yale French Studies*, XXV (1960), 65–71.

[4] Jean-Paul Sartre, "Albert Camus," *France Observateur*, January 7, 1960, p. 17.

[5] See Norman Rudich, "Individual as Myth," *Chicago Review*, XIII (Summer, 1959), 109.

[6] Viggiani, "Camus and the Fall from Innocence," p. 67.

[7] Maurice Blanchot, "La Confession dédaigneuse," *La Nouvelle Nouvelle Revue Française*, VIII (December 1956), 1050–1053.

[8] Brée, *Camus*, p. 110.

[9] Paul Ginestier, *La Pensée de Camus* (n.p.: Bordas, 1964), p. 204.

[10] The English quotations are taken from *The Fall*, tr. Justin O'Brien (New York: Vintage Books, 1956); page number references are to this edition and follow the quotations in parentheses.

[11] For the *height* images in Camus' *La Chute*, see Stephen Ullmann, *The Image in the Modern French Novel* (Cambridge, England: The University Press, 1960), pp. 239–299.

[12] Marcel Arland, "*La Chute* d'Albert Camus," *La Nouvelle Nouvelle Revue Française*, VIII (July 1956), 125.

[13] William R. Mueller, *The Prophetic Voice in Modern Fiction* (New York: Association Press, 1959), p. 57.

[14] Viggiani, "Camus and the Fall from Innocence," p. 69.

[15] For a good account of the origin of the quarrel, see Nicola Chiaromonte, "Sartre versus Camus: A Political Quarrel," *Partisan Review*, XIX (November-December 1952), 680–687; this article has been reprinted in *Camus*, ed. G. Brée (Englewood Cliffs, N.J.: Prentice-Hall, 1962), pp. 31–37. For an analysis of the allusions to Sartre and the existentialists in *La Chute*, see in particular Adele King. "Structure and Meaning in *La Chute*," PMLA, LXXVII (December 1962), 661–664; Richard Lehan, "Levels of Reality in the Novels of Albert Camus," *Modern Fiction Studies*, X (Autumn, 1964), 240–241.

[16] Brée, *Camus*, pp. 106–109, 132–134.

[17] For this kind of interpretation, see Victor Brombert, " 'The Renegade' or the Terror of the Absolute," *Yale French Studies*, XXV (1960), 81–84, and Brombert, *The Intellectual Hero: Studies in the French Novel, 1880–1955* (Philadelphia: J. B. Lippincott, 1961), pp. 227–231.

[18] Anne Minor, "The Short Stories of Albert Camus," *Yale French Studies*, XXV (1960), 77.

[19] *The Myth of Sisyphus and Other Essays*, tr. Justin O'Brien (New York: Vintage Books, 1955), p. 50.

[20] Franck Jotterand, "Entretien avec Albert Camus," *La Gazette de Lausanne*, March 27–28, 1954.

[21] For *the city as image of man*, see Jacob Isaacs, *An Assessment of Twentieth Century Literature* (London: Secker and Warburg, 1951), pp. 55–58.

[22] See R. Theis, "Albert Camus' Rückkehr zu Sisyphus," *Romanische Forschungen*, LXX (1958), 66–90.

[23] *The Plague*, tr. Stuart Gilbert (New York: Modern Library, 1948), p. 175.

[24] André Nicolas, *Une Philosophie de l'existence: Albert Camus* (Paris: Presses Universitaires de France, 1964), p. 167.

[25] *Caligula and Three Other Plays*, tr. Stuart Gilbert (New York: Vintage Books, 1958), pp. 170–173.

[26] For excellent studies of the relationship between *La Chute* and Dante's *Inferno*, see Alfred Galpin, "Italian Echoes in Albert Camus: Two Notes on *La Chute*," *Symposium*, XII (1958), 65–72; Adele King, "Structure and Meaning in *La Chute*," pp. 664–667; Carina Gadourek, *Les Innocents et les coupables; Essai d'exégèse de l'oeuvre d'Albert Camus* (The Hague: Mouton, 1963), pp. 176–187.

[27] Leon S. Roudiez, "*L'Etranger, La Chute*, and the Aesthetic Legacy of Gide," *The French Review*, XXXII (February 1959), 308.

[28] See Gerald Stourzh, "The Unforgivable Sin: An Interpretation of *The Fall*," *Chicago Review*, XV (Summer 1961), 45–57, for a discussion of the sin against the Holy Ghost as central theme of *The Fall*.

[29] Acts 10:42–43.

[30] *The Rebel*, tr. and rev. by Anthony Bower (New York: Vintage Books, 1956), p. 33.

[31] *Ibid.*, p. 67.

[32] Cruickshank, *Camus*, p. 187.

[33] Rachel Bespaloff, "The World of the Man Condemned to Death," in *Camus*, ed. G. Brée (New York: Harcourt, Brace and World, 1964) p. 103.

[34] Brée, *Camus*, p. 132.

Dostoevsky's The Possessed

[1] See also Peter M. Axthelm, *The Modern Confessional Novel* (New Haven: Yale University Press, 1967), pp. 13–96. Emmanuel Berl, "Face à l'absurde," *La Table Ronde*, CXLVI (February 1960), 163–166. Charles B. Brockmann, "Metamorphoses of Hell: The Spiritual Quandary in *La Chute*," *French Review*, XXXV (February 1962), 361–368. Garrett Green, *A Kingdom Not of This World* (Stanford: Stanford University Press, 1964). Jacques Madaule, "Camus et Dostoievski," *La Table Ronde*, CXLVI (February 1960), 127–136. René Micha, "L'Agneau dans le placard," *La Nouvelle Nouvelle Revue Française*, XV (March 1960), 501–505. H. G. Schogt, *La Solitude du souterrain* (The Hague: Mouton, 1958). Sara Toenes, "Public Confession in *La Chute*," *Wisconsin Studies in Contemporary Literature*, IV (Autumn, 1963), 305–318.

[2] *The Stranger*, tr. Stuart Gilbert (New York: Vintage Books, 1954), p. 80.

[3] Fyodor Dostoevsky, *The Brothers Karamazov*, tr. Constance Garnett (New York: Modern Library, 1929), XII, v, p. 864. All other references are to this edition.

[4] *Ibid.*, V, iv, p. 229.

[5] *Ibid.*, V, iii, p. 283.

[6] Fyodor Dostoevsky, *The Idiot*, tr. Constance Garnett, rev. John W. Strahan (New York: Washington Square Press, 1965), III, v, p. 403. All other references are to this edition.

[7] *The Brothers Karamazov*, II, vi, p. 81.

[8] *The Myth of Sisyphus and Other Essays*, tr. Justin O'Brien (New York: Vintage Books, 1955), p. 50.

[9] Albert Camus, "The Other Russia," *New York Herald Tribune*, December 19, 1957.

[10] *The Myth of Sisyphus*, p. 82.

[11] Madaule, "Camus et Dostoëvski," pp. 127–128.

[12] Albert Camus, *Carnets, Mai 1935–Mars 1951* (Paris: Imprimérie Nationale, 1962–1964), pp. 85, 231.

[13] Albert Camus, "Foreword" to *The Possessed*, tr. Justin O'Brien (New York: Vintage Books, 1964), no page numbers. Note: The "Foreword" does not appear in the Gallimard edition.

[14] Warren Ramsey, "Albert Camus on Capital Punishment: His Adaptation of *The Possessed*," *Yale Review*, XLVIII (Summer, 1959), 634.

[15] *Ibid.*, p. 636.

[16] Fyodor Dostoevsky, *The Possessed*, tr. Constance Garnett (New York: Modern Library, 1936). Stavrogin's twenty-four hour presence covers 104 pages; the transitional eight-day lapse 64; and the "big scene" (including "Stavrogin's Confession") 332; the Modern Library edition (excluding the "Variant Readings") contains 730 pages of which the Stepan Trofimovitch frame-of-reference story covers a little over 200. Stavrogin's presence or influence indeed covers most pages of the "internal" novel. (Part, chapter, and page references, appearing within the text, are to this edition.)

[17] Joseph W. Beach, *The Twentieth Century Novel* (New York: Appleton-Century, 1932), pp. 155–163.

[18] Vyacheslav Ivanov, *Freedom and the Tragic Life: A Study in Dostoevsky* (New York: Noonday Press, 1952), pp. 11–15.

[19] George Steiner, *Tolstoy or Dostoevsky* (New York: Vintage Books, 1961), pp. 137–160. Also see Camus, "Foreword" to *The Possessed*; René Fülöp-Miller and Friedrich Eckstein, *Der unbekannte Dostojewski* (München: R. Piper, 1926), p. 133.

[20] Constantin Motchoulski, *Dostoievski, l'homme et l'oeuvre*, tr. G. Welter (Paris: Payot, 1963), pp. 362–365.

[21] Fyodor Dostoevsky, *The Diary of a Writer*, tr. and annotated by Boris Brasol (New York: Charles Scribner's Sons, 1949), I, 149.

[22] Ivanov, *Freedom and the Tragic Life*, pp. 61–64.

[23] Steiner, *Tolstoy or Dostoevsky*, pp. 311, 314.

[24] Robert Payne, *Dostoyevsky: A Human Portrait* (New York: Alfred Knopf, 1961), p. 261.

[25] Ralph J. Hallman, *Psychology of Literature: A Study of Alienation and Tragedy* (New York: Philosophical Library, 1961), pp. 206–223; Renato Poggioli, "Dostoevski, or Reality and Myth," in *The Phoenix and the Spider* (Cambridge: Harvard University Press, 1957), pp. 16–32; Leon A. Zander, *Dostoevsky*, tr. Natalie Duddington (London: SCM Press, 1948), pp. 99 ff.

[26] Irving Howe, *Politics and the Novel* (New York: Meridian Books, 1957), p. 64.

[27] Richard Curle, *Characters of Dostoievsky: Studies from Four Novels* (London: W. Heinemann, 1950), p. 138.

[28] Fülöp-Miller and Eckstein, *Der unbekannte Dostojewski*, p. 130.

[29] F. H. Dostoievsky, *Les Démons; Carnets des démons*, tr. B. de Schloezer et S. Luneau (Paris: Gallimard [Pléiade éd.], 1955), pp. 784, 787.

[30] *Ibid.*, p. 1051. Entry for June 9, 1870.

[31] *Ibid.*, p. 1069. Entry for May 23, 1870.

[32] *Diary of a Writer*, I, 245. Entry for March 1876.

[33] *The Brothers Karamazov*, VI, iii, p. 400.

[34] Janko Lavrin, *Dostoevsky and His Creation: A Psycho-Critical Study* (London: Collins, 1920), pp. 111–114; Henri Troyat, *Dostoievsky* (Paris: Librairie Arthème Fayard, 1940), pp. 125, 370.

[35] Nicholas Berdyaev, *Dostoevsky* (New York: Meridian Books, 1957), p. 76.

[36] For a discussion of animal symbolism in Dostoevsky, see Ralph E. Matlaw, "Recurrent Imagery in Dostoevskij," *Harvard Slavic Studies*, III (1957), 201–225.

[37] Dostoevsky, *The Idiot*, III, vi, p. 418.

[38] *The Brothers Karamazov*, XI, ix, pp. 815–816.

[39] I have assumed that the originally suppressed chapter "At Tihon's," also known as "Stavrogin's Confession," belongs, as Dostoevsky intended when he wrote the novel, in Part II, between chapters VIII and IX.

[40] E. J. Simmons in *Dostoievsky: The Making of a Novelist* (New York: Vintage Books, 1962), pp. 252–253, has remarked that Stavrogin's eventual refusal to publish his confession in fear of ridicule "is symbolic of his ultimate spiritual bankruptcy."

[41] Zander, *Dostoevsky*, p. 13.

[42] Berdyaev, *Dostoevsky*, pp. 41–44. Dmitri Chizhevsky, "The Theme of the Double in Dostoevsky," in *Dostoevsky*, ed. René Wellek (Englewood Cliffs, N.J.: Prentice Hall, 1962), p. 118. Pavel N. Evdokimov, *Der Abstieg in die Hölle; Gogol und Dostojewskij* (Salzburg: Otto Müller, 1965), pp. 234–235. Romano Guardini, *Religiöse Gestalten in Dostojewskijs Werk* (München: Kösel Verlag, 1951), p. 291. Motchoulski, *Dostoievski, L'homme et l'oeuvre*,

122 NOTES TO PP. 86–92

pp. 361–362, 376. Avraham Yarmolinsky, *Dostoevsky, His Life and Art* (2nd ed., revised and enlarged; New York: Criterion Books, 1957), pp. 292–294.
[43] Berdyaev, *Dostoevsky*, pp. 112–113. Ivanov, *Freedom and the Tragic Life*, pp. 42, 60–63. Payne, *Dostoyevsky*, pp. 267–271. Nathan Rosen, "Chaos and Dostoevsky's Women," *Kenyon Review*, XX (Spring, 1958), 257–277. Zander, *Dostoevsky*, pp. 66–137.
[44] Some commentators consider *The Possessed* primarily a political tract. See, for example, Joseph Bohatec, *Der Imperialismusgedanke und die Lebensphilosophie Dostojewskijs* (Graz-Köln: H. Böhlaus Nachf., 1951); Howe, *Politics and the Novel*, pp. 51–75; Stanislaw Mackiewicz, *Dostoyevsky* (London: Orbis, 1947); Arthur McDowall, "*The Possessed* and Bolshevism," *London Mercury*, XVII (November 1927), 52–61; Charles A. Moser, *Antinihilism in the Russian Novel of the 1860's* (The Hague: Mouton, 1964); Philip Rahv, "Dostoevski and Politics: Notes on *The Possessed*," *Partisan Review*, V (July 1938), 25–36.
[45] Nina Gourfinkel, *Dostoievski, notre contemporain* (Paris: Calmann-Lévy, 1961), p. 241.
[46] For *The Possessed* as a religious discourse, see Evdokimov, *Der Abstieg in die Hölle*, pp. 229 ff.; René Girard, "Métaphysique du souterrain dans les possédés," *La Table Ronde*, CLXXXIII (April 1963), 73–76; Guardini, *Religiöse Gestalten in Dostojewskijs Werk*; Paul Ramsey, "God's Grace and Man's Guilt," *Journal of Religion*, XXXI (January 1951), 21–37; George C. Strem, "The Moral World of Dostoevsky," *Russian Review*, XVI (July 1957), 15–26.
[47] Berdyaev, *Dostoevsky*, p. 203.
[48] Dostoievsky, *Les Démons; Carnets des démons*, tr. B. de Schloezer et S. Luneau (Paris: Gallimard, 1955), p. 825. Entry for March 11, 1870.

Melville's Moby-Dick

[1] Philarète Chasles failed to bring Melville to public attention in *Journal des débats* (1846) and *Revue des deux mondes* (1849). Not until 1919 (the date of the Melville centennial) did he come to the fore in France. See Felix Ansermoz-Dubois, *L'Interprétation française de la littérature américaine d'entre-deux-guerres* (Lausanne: Imprimerie de la Concorde, 1944), p. 8. *Poor Folk* was published in 1846; three years later Dostoevsky was deported.
[2] John C. Fiske in "Herman Melville in Soviet Criticism," *Comparative Literature*, V (Winter, 1953), 31–32, states: "The earliest Soviet critical study of Melville that I have discovered appears in the *Literary Encyclopaedia* [1930–1939; Vol. VII, pp. 108–109] over the signature of A. Meleshko."

[3] Merton M. Sealts, *Melville's Reading: A Check-list of Books owned and Borrowed* (Madison: University of Wisconsin Press, 1966).

[4] Albert Camus, *Carnets, Mai 1935–Mars 1951* (Paris: Imprimerie Nationale, 1962–1964), pp. 150, 153, 155, 342–343.

[5] Albert Camus, *The Myth of Sisyphus and Other Essays*, tr. Justin O'Brien (New York: Vintage Books, 1955), p. 83.

[6] Albert Camus, "Herman Melville," in *Les Ecrevains célèbres*, ed. Raymond Queneau (Paris: Lucien Mazenod, 1953), III, 128.

[7] Leon S. Roudiez, "Camus and *Moby-Dick*," *Symposium*, XV (Spring, 1961), 30–40. See also his "Strangers in Melville and Camus," *The French Review*, XXXI (January 1958), 217–226.

[8] The term "dramatic" is here used in a technical sense and refers to any or all of such devices as division into acts, unities of time and place, italicized stage directions, set speeches with the speaker named in capitals, soliloquies, and dialogues without commentary.

[9] Herman Melville, "Hawthorne and His Mosses," in *Herman Melville*, ed. Willard Thorp (New York: American Book, 1938), p. 334 (originally published in *The Literary World*, August 17 and 24, 1850).

[10] Charles Olson, *Call Me Ishmael* (New York: Reynal and Hitchcock, 1947), pp. 66–69.

[11] Newton Arvin, *Herman Melville* (New York: William Sloane Associates, 1950), pp. 154–158.

[12] Milton Millhauser, "The Form of *Moby-Dick*," *The Journal of Aesthetics and Art Criticism*, XIII (June 1955), 527–532. Henry A. Myers, "Captain Ahab's Discovery: The Tragic Meaning of *Moby-Dick*," *New England Quarterly*, XV (March 1942), 15–34. Charles Olson, "Melville et Shakespeare, ou la découverte de *Moby-Dick*," *Les Temps Modernes*, VII (October 1951), 647–676. Jean Simon, *Herman Melville, marin, métaphysicien, et poète* (Paris: Boivin, 1939), pp. 334–341. Dan Vogel, "The Dramatic Chapters in *Moby-Dick*," *Nineteenth Century Fiction*, XIII (December 1958), 239–247. André Le Vot, "Shakespeare et Melville: Le Thème impérial dans *Moby-Dick*," *Etudes Anglaises*, XVII (October–December 1964), 549–563.

[13] Charles Feidelson, Jr., *Symbolism and American Literature* (Chicago: University of Chicago Press, 1953), p. 31.

[14] Gerhard Friedrich, *In Pursuit of Moby-Dick: Melville's Image of Man* (Wallingford, Pa.: Pendle Hill, 1958), p. 5.

[15] Richard V. Chase, *Herman Melville* (New York: Macmillan, 1949), p. 73.

[16] Feidelson, *Symbolism*, p. 32.

[17] Howard P. Vincent, *The Trying-out of Moby-Dick* (Boston: Houghton Mifflin, 1949), p. 56.

[18] Hans Helmcke, *Die Funktion des Ich-Erzählers in Herman*

124

Melvilles Roman Moby-Dick (München: Max Hueber, 1957), pp. 131–133.

[19] Alfred Kazin, "Ishmael and Ahab," *The Atlantic Monthly,* CXCVIII (November 1956), 82–83.

[20] Paul Brodtkorb, *Ishmael's White World* (New Haven: Yale University Press, 1965), p. 3.

[21] Maurice Friedman, *Problematic Rebel* (New York: Random House, 1963), p. 59.

[22] Marius Bewley in *The Eccentric Design* (London: Chatto and Windus, 1959) suggests that an apparently loose form in *Moby-Dick* is brought about because Melville's heroes are "incapable of development or progression." They are "trapped in the endless unfolding of moral ambiguities whose total significance was to drain all possible meaning from life. Reality which is conceived as endlessly ambiguous, never coming to rest in any certainty, is the negation of form" (pp. 191–192).

[23] Herman Melville, *Moby-Dick or the Whale,* ed. Luther S. Mansfield and Howard P. Vincent (New York: Hendricks House, 1952). All other chapter and page number references are to this edition.

[24] Friedrich, *In Pursuit of Moby-Dick,* p. 13.

[25] "Explanatory Notes" to the Mansfield and Vincent edition of *Moby-Dick or the Whale,* p. 631.

[26] *The Letters of Herman Melville,* ed. Merrell R. Davis and William H. Gilman (New Haven: Yale University Press, 1960), pp. 124–125.

[27] Arvin, *Herman Melville,* pp. 162–163.

[28] Henry F. Pommer, *Milton and Melville* (Pittsburgh: University of Pittsburgh Press, 1950).

[29] Daniel G. Hoffman, "Myth, Magic, and Metaphor in *Moby-Dick,*" in his *Form and Fable in American Fiction* (New York: Oxford University Press, 1961), p. 234.

[30] Henry A. Murray, "In Nomine Diaboli," in Tyrus Hillway and Luther S. Mansfield, eds., *Moby-Dick Centennial Essays* (Dallas: Southern Methodist University Press, 1953), p. 10.

[31] Rudolf Sühnel, "Melvilles *Moby-Dick:* Versuch einer Deutung," *Die Neuere Sprachen,* V (1956), 560.

[32] Lawrance Thompson, *Melville's Quarrel with God* (Princeton: Princeton University Press, 1952), p. 179.

[33] Roudiez, "Strangers in Melville and Camus," pp. 222–223.

[34] R. P. Adams, "Romanticism and the American Renaissance," *American Literature,* XXIII (January 1952), 422.

[35] William Hubben, "Ahab, the Whaling Quaker," *Religion in Life,* XVIII (Summer 1949), 372.

[36] James Baird, *Ishmael* (Baltimore: Johns Hopkins Press, 1956), p. 251.

[37] Lewis Mumford, *Herman Melville* (New York: Harcourt, Brace, 1929), p. 158.

[38] Herman Melville, *Redburn: His First Voyage* (Garden City, N.Y.: Doubleday [Anchor Books], 1957), XII, 53–60.

[39] Herman Melville, *White Jacket*, Introduction by William Plower (New York: Grove Press, 1952), XXXIX, 162; XIX, 85–86.

[40] Herman Melville, *Mardi* (Boston: The St. Botolph Society, 1923), LIV, 146; I, 3; CLXXXV, 579; CLXXXV, 548.

[41] Henry A. Murray, "Introduction" to Herman Melville, *Pierre or the Ambiguities* (New York: Farrar, Strauss, 1949), pp. xiv-xv.

[42] Melville, *Pierre*, XIX, ii, 321.

[43] Herman Melville, *Billy Budd, Sailor*, ed. Harrison Hayford and Merton M. Sealts (Chicago: University of Chicago Press, 1962), I, 49; II, 52; XIX, 98.

[44] It is interesting to note that Ahab not only has an ivory leg, but also possesses an ivory stool (XXX, 126) and an ivory-inlaid dinner table (XXXIV, 147). Most important, perhaps, in this respect is the reference to Ahab's ship as the "ivory Pequod" (LI, 230).

[45] Chase, *Herman Melville*, p. 97.

[46] John Bernstein, *Pacifism and Rebellion in the Writings of Herman Melville* (The Hague: Mouton, 1964), p. 104.

[47] William Braswell, *Melville's Religious Thought* (Durham, N.C.: Duke University Press, 1943), p. 60.

[48] Dorothee Grdseloff, "A Note on the Origin of Fedallah in *Moby-Dick*," *American Literature*, XXVII (November 1955), 396–403. She writes that, given the Arabian meaning, Fedallah would then mean "one who sacrifices himself for God" and would symbolize the "destroying angel" sent by God to bring about the "assassination" of Ahab, the heretic. In the accomplishment of his mission Fedallah, the mystic, offers up his life and thus becomes a *feda*, a "sacrifice" or "ransom" (p. 403).

[49] Arvin, *Herman Melville*, p. 192.

[50] M. O. Percival, *A Reading of Moby-Dick* (Chicago: University of Chicago Press, 1950), p. 39. See also Baird, *Ishmael*, pp. 280–281.

[51] For interesting commentary on the fire and light symbolisms in *Moby-Dick*, see Bernstein, *Pacifism and Rebellion*, pp. 100–103; Max Frank, *Die Farb- und Lichtsymbolik im Prosawerk Herman Melvilles* (Heidelberg: Carl Winter, 1967), pp. 106–110; Paul W. Miller, "Sun and Fire in Melville's *Moby-Dick*," *Nineteenth Century Fiction*, XIII (September 1958), 139–144; Charles C. Walcutt, "The Fire Symbolism in *Moby-Dick*," *Modern Language Notes*, LIX (April 1944), 304–310.

[52] Arvin, *Herman Melville*, pp. 188–189. See also Braswell, *Melville's Religious Thought*, p. 59; Chase, *Herman Melville*, pp. 49–51;

Hoffman, "Myth, Magic, and Metaphor in *Moby-Dick*," p. 271; Mumford, *Herman Melville*, p. 185.

[53] For a most thorough study of Melville's use of "white" symbolism, see Frank, *Die Farb- und Lichtsymbolik im Prosawerk Herman Melvilles*; for a literary parallel, see the concluding chapter of Edgar A. Poe, "The *Narrative of A. Gordon Pym*," in *Complete Works*, ed. James A. Harrison (New York: Thomas Y. Crowell, 1902), III, 5–242.

[54] For pertinent commentary on the function of the "gams" in the novel, see Don Geiger, "Melville's Black God: Contrary Evidence in the Town-Ho's Story," *American Literature*, XXV (January 1954), 464–471; Bruce I. Granger, "The Gams in *Moby-Dick*," *Western Humanities Review*, VIII (Winter, 1953–54), 41–47; James D. Young, "The Nine Gams of the 'Pequod,'" *American Literature*, XXV (January 1954) 449–463.

Bibliography

Primary Sources

Beckett, Samuel. *Waiting for Godot*. New York: Grove Press, 1954.
Camus, Albert. *Actuelles I; Chroniques 1944–1948*. Paris: Gallimard, 1950.
Camus, Albert. *Caligula and Three Other Plays*. Tr. Stuart Gilbert. New York: Vintage Books, 1958.
Camus, Albert. *Exile and the Kingdom*. Tr. Justin O'Brien. New York: Vintage Books, 1957.
Camus, Albert. *The Fall*. Tr. Justin O'Brien. New York: Vintage Books, 1956.
Camus, Albert. *The Myth of Sisyphus and Other Essays*. Tr. Justin O'Brien. New York: Vintage Books, 1955.
Camus, Albert. *Noces*. Paris: Editions Charlot, 1937.
Camus, Albert. *Notebooks 1935–1942*. Tr. Philip Thody. New York: Modern Library, 1965.
Camus, Albert. *Notebooks 1942–1951*. Tr. Justin O'Brien. New York: Alfred Knopf, 1965.
Camus, Albert. *The Plague*. Tr. Stuart Gilbert. New York: Modern Library, 1948.
Camus, Albert. *The Possessed*. Tr. Justin O'Brien. New York: Vintage Books, 1964.
Camus, Albert. *The Rebel*. Tr. and rev. by Anthony Bower. New York: Vintage Books, 1956.
Camus, Albert. *The Stranger*. Tr. Stuart Gilbert. New York: Vintage Books, 1954.

Céline, Louis-Ferdinand. *Journey to the End of Night*. Tr. John H. P. Marks. London: Penguin Books, 1966.

Dostoevsky, Fyodor. *The Brothers Karamazov*. Tr. Constance Garnett. New York: Modern Library, 1929.

Dostoevsky, Fyodor. *Les Démons; Carnets des démons*. Tr. B. de Schloezer et S. Luneau. Paris: Gallimard (Pléiade éd.), 1955.

Dostoevsky, Fyodor. *The Diary of a Writer*. Tr. Boris Brasol. 2 Vols. New York: Charles Scribner's Sons, 1949.

Dostoevsky, Fyodor. *The Idiot*. Tr. Constance Garnett; rev. John W. Strahan. New York: Washington Square Press, 1965.

Dostoevsky, Fyodor. *The Possessed*. Tr. Constance Garnett. New York: Modern Library, 1936.

Eliot, Thomas S. *Murder in the Cathedral*, in *The Complete Poems and Plays: 1909–1950*. New York: Harcourt, Brace and World, 1952. Pp. 173–221.

Kafka, Franz. *Amerika*. Tr. Edwin Muir. New York: Modern Library, 1956.

Kafka, Franz. *The Castle*. Tr. Edwin Muir. New York: Alfred Knopf, 1954.

Kafka, Franz. *The Trial*. Tr. Edwin Muir. Garden City, N.Y.: Doubleday, 1955.

Malraux, André. *The Conquerors*. Tr. Winifred S. Whale. Boston: Beacon Press, 1956.

Malraux, André. *Days of Wrath*. Tr. Haakon M. Chevalier. New York: Random House, 1936.

Malraux, André. *Man's Fate*. Tr. Haakon M. Chevalier. New York: Modern Library, 1934.

Malraux, André. *Man's Hope*. Tr. Stuart Gilbert and Alastair Macdonald. New York: Random House, 1938.

Malraux, André. *The Royal Way*. Tr. Stuart Gilbert. New York: Vintage Books, 1955.

Malraux, André, *The Temptation of the West*. Tr. Robert Hollander. New York: Vintage Books, 1961.

Melville, Herman. *Billy Budd, Sailor*. Ed. Harrison Hayford and Merton M. Sealts. Chicago: University of Chicago Press, 1962.

Melville, Herman. *The Letters of Herman Melville*. Ed. Merrell R. Davis and William H. Gilman. New Haven: Yale University Press, 1960.

Melville, Herman. *Mardi*. Boston: The St. Botolph Society, 1923.

Melville, Herman. *Moby-Dick or the Whale*. Ed. Luther S. Mansfield and Howard P. Vincent. New York: Hendricks House, 1952.

Melville, Herman. *Pierre or the Ambiguities*. Ed. Henry A. Murray. New York: Farrar, Strauss, 1949.

Melville, Herman. *Redburn: His First Voyage*. Garden City, N.Y.: Doubleday (Anchor Books), 1957.

Melville, Herman. *White Jacket.* Introduction by William Plower. New York: Grove Press, 1952.

Nietzsche, Friedrich. *The Birth of Tragedy.* Tr. W. A. Haussmann. Vol. I of *The Complete Works of Friedrich Nietzsche.* Ed. Oscar Levy. 18 vols. London: T. N. Foulis, 1909.

Nietzsche, Friedrich. *The Joyful Wisdom.* Tr. Thomas Common. Vol. X of *The Complete Works of Friedrich Nietzsche.* Ed. Oscar Levy. 18 vols. London: T. N. Foulis, 1910.

Poe, Edgar A. *The Narrative of A. Gordon Pym.* Vol. III of *Complete Works.* 17 vols. Ed. James A. Harrison. New York: Thomas Y. Crowell, 1902. Pp. 5–242.

Sartre, Jean-Paul. *The Flies.* Tr. Stuart Gilbert. New York: Alfred Knopf, 1947.

Secondary Sources

Adams, R. P. "Romanticism and the American Renaissance," *American Literature,* XXIII (January 1952), 419–432.

Ansermoz-Dubois, Felix. *L'Interprétation française de la littérature américaine d'entre-deux-guerres (1919–1939); Essai de bibliographie.* Lausanne: Imprimerie de la Concorde, 1944.

Arendt, Hannah. "Franz Kafka: A Revaluation," *Partisan Review,* XI (Fall 1944), 412–422.

Arland, Marcel. "La Chute d'Albert Camus," *La Nouvelle Nouvelle Revue Française,* VIII (July 1956), 123–127.

Arland, Marcel. "Sur un nouveau Mal du Siècle," *La Nouvelle Revue Française,* XXII (February 1924), 149–158.

Arvin, Newton. *Herman Melville.* New York: William Sloane Associates, 1950.

Axthelm, Peter M. *The Modern Confessional Novel.* New Haven: Yale University Press, 1967.

Baird, James. *Ishmael.* Baltimore: Johns Hopkins Press, 1956.

Baudelaire, Charles. "The Salon of 1846," in *Art in Paris: 1845–1862; Salons and Other Exhibitions.* Tr. and ed. J. Mayne. London: Phaidon Press, 1965. Pp. 41–120.

Beach, Joseph W. *The Twentieth Century Novel.* New York: Appleton-Century, 1932.

Berdyaev, Nicholas. *Dostoevsky.* New York: Meridian Books, 1957.

Berl, Emmanuel. "Face à l'absurde," *La Table Ronde,* CXLVI (February 1960), 163–166.

Bernstein, John. *Pacifism and Rebellion in the Writings of Herman Melville.* The Hague: Mouton, 1964.

Bespaloff, Rachel. "Les Carrefours de Camus; Le Monde du condamné à mort," *Esprit,* XVIII (January 1950), 1–26.

Bespaloff, Rachel. "The World of Man Condemned to Death," in

Camus, ed. G. Bree. New York: Harcourt, Brace and World, 1964. Pp. 92–107.

Bewley, Marius. The Eccentric Design. London: Chatto and Windus, 1959.

Blanchot, Maurice. "La Confession dédaigneuse," La Nouvelle Nouvelle Revue Française, VIII (December 1956), 1050–1056.

Bohatec, Joseph. Der Imperialismusgedanke und die Lebensphilosophie Dostojewskijs. Graz-Köln: H. Böhlaus Nachf., 1951.

Braswell, William. Melville's Religious Thought. Durham, N.C.: Duke University Press, 1943.

Brée, Germaine. Camus. Rev. ed. New York: Harcourt, Brace and World, 1964.

Brochmann, Charles B. "Metamorphoses of Hell: The Spiritual Quandary in La Chute," French Review, XXXV (February 1962), 361–368.

Brod, Max. Franz Kafka; eine Biographie. Berlin: S. Fischer Verlag, 1954.

Brod, Max. "Nachwort zur ersten Ausgabe," in Franz Kafka, Das Schloss. New York: Schocken Books, 1946. Pp. 415–424.

Brodtkorb, Paul. Ishmael's White World. New Haven: Yale University Press, 1965.

Brombert, Victor. The Intellectual Hero: Studies in the French Novel, 1880–1955. Philadelphia: J. B. Lippincott, 1961.

Brombert, Victor. " 'The Renegade' or the Terror of the Absolute," Yale French Studies, XXV (1960), 81–84.

Camus, Albert. "Foreword" to The Possessed. Tr. Justin O'Brien. New York: Vintage Books, 1964.

Camus, Albert. "Herman Melville," Les Ecrivains célèbres. Vol. III. Ed. Raymond Queneau. Paris: Lucien Mazenod, 1953. Pp. 128–129.

Camus, Albert. "Hope and the Absurd in the Work of Franz Kafka," in The Myth of Sisyphus and Other Essays. Tr. Justin O'Brien. New York: Vintage Books, 1955. Pp. 92–102.

Camus Albert. "Lettre au directeur des Temps Modernes," Les Temps Modernes, VIII (August 1952), 317–333.

Camus, Albert. "The Other Russia," New York Herald Tribune, December 19, 1957.

Chase, Richard V. Herman Melville. New York: Macmillan, 1949.

Chiaromonte, Nicola. "Sartre versus Camus: A Political Quarrel," Partisan Review, XIX (November-December 1952), 680–687.

Chizhevsky, Dmitri. "The Theme of the Double in Dostoevsky," in Dostoevsky. Ed. René Wellek. Englewood Cliffs, N.J.: Prentice-Hall, 1962. Pp. 112–129.

Cruickshank, John. Albert Camus and the Literature of Revolt. New York: Oxford University Press, 1960.

Curle, Richard. *Characters of Dostoievsky: Studies from Four Novels.* London: W. Heinemann, 1950.

Evdokimov, Pavel N. *Der Abstieg in die Hölle; Gogol und Dostojewskij.* Salzburg: Otto Müller, 1965.

Feidelson, Charles, Jr. *Symbolism and American Literature.* Chicago: University of Chicago Press, 1953.

Fiske, John C. "Herman Melville in Soviet Criticism," *Comparative Literature,* V (Winter 1953), 30–39.

Fowlie, Wallace. *Age of Surrealism.* Bloomington: Indiana University Press, 1960.

Frank, Max. *Die Farb- und Lichtsymbolik im Prosawerk Herman Melvilles.* Heidelberg: Carl Winter, 1967.

Friedman, Maurice. *Problematic Rebel.* New York: Random House, 1963.

Friedrich, Gerhard. *In Pursuit of Moby-Dick: Melville's Image of Man.* Wallingford, Pa.: Pendle Hill, 1958.

Frye, Northrop. *Anatomy of Criticism.* Princeton: Princeton University Press, 1957.

Fülöp-Miller, René, and Friedrich Eckstein. *Der unbekannte Dostojewski.* München: R. Piper, 1926.

Fürst, Norbert. *Die offenen Geheimtüren Franz Kafkas.* Heidelberg: Wolfgang Rothe Verlag, 1956.

Gadourek, Carina. *Les Innocents et les coupables; Essai d'exégèse de l'oeuvre d'Albert Camus.* The Hague: Mouton, 1963.

Galpin, Alfred. "Italian Echoes in Albert Camus: Two Notes on *La Chute*," *Symposium,* XII (1958), 65–79.

Geiger, Don. "Melville's Black God: Contrary Evidence in the Town-Ho's Story," *American Literature,* XXV (January 1954), 464–471.

Ginestier, Paul. *La Pensée de Camus.* N.p.: Bordas, 1964.

Girard, René. *Mensonge romantique et vérité romanesque.* Paris: B. Grasset, 1961.

Girard, René. "Métaphysique du souterrain dans les possédés," *La Table Ronde,* CLXXXIII (April 1963), 73–76.

Gourfinkel, Nina. *Dostoievski, notre contemporain.* Paris: Calmann-Lévy, 1961.

Granger, Bruce I. "The Gams in *Moby-Dick*," *Western Humanities Review,* VIII (Winter 1953–54), 41–47.

Grdseloff, Dorothee. "A Note on the Origin of Fedallah in *Moby-Dick*," *American Literature,* XXVII (November 1955), 396–403.

Green, Garrett. *A Kingdom Not of This World.* Stanford: Stanford University Press, 1964.

Guardini, Romano. *Religiöse Gestalten in Dostojewskijs Werk: Studien über den Glauben.* München: Kösel Verlag, 1951.

Hallman, Ralph J. *Psychology of Literature: A Study of Alienation and Tragedy.* New York: Philosophical Library, 1961.

Heller, Erich. "The World of Franz Kafka," in *The Disinherited Mind.* London: Bowes and Bowes, 1957. Pp. 199–231.

Helmcke, Hans. *Die Funktion des Ich-Erzählers in Herman Melvilles Roman Moby-Dick.* München: Max Hueber, 1957.

Hocke, Gustav R. *Die Welt als Labyrinth.* Vol. II. 2 vols. Hamburg: Rowohlt, 1959.

Hoffman, Daniel G. "Myth, Magic, and Metaphor in *Moby-Dick,*" in *Form and Fable in American Fiction.* New York: Oxford University Press, 1961. Pp. 233–278.

Howe, Irving. "Dostoevsky: The Politics of Salvation," in *Politics and the Novel.* New York: Meridian Books, 1957. Pp. 51–75.

Hubben, William. "Ahab, the Whaling Quaker," *Religion in Life,* XVIII (Summer 1949), 363–373.

Isaacs, Jacob. *An Assessment of Twentieth Century Literature.* London: Secker and Warburg, 1951.

Ivanov, Vyacheslav. *Freedom and the Tragic Life: A Study in Dostoevsky.* New York: Noonday Press, 1952.

Jotterand, Franck. "Entretien avec Albert Camus," *La Gazette de Lausanne,* March 27–28, 1954.

Kahler, Erich. "The Transformation of Modern Fiction," *Comparative Literature,* VII (1955), 121–128.

Kazin, Alfred. "Ishmael and Ahab," *The Atlantic Monthly,* CXCVIII (November 1956), 81–85.

King, Adele. "Structure and Meaning in *La Chute,*" *PMLA,* LXXVII (December 1962), 660–667.

Krieger, Murray. *The Tragic Vision.* Chicago: University of Chicago Press (Phoenix Book), 1960.

Lavrin, Janko. *Dostoevsky and His Creation: A Psycho-Critical Study.* London: Collins, 1920.

Lehan, Richard. "Levels of Reality in the Novels of Albert Camus," *Modern Fiction Studies,* X (Autumn 1964), 232–244.

McDowall, Arthur. "*The Possessed* and Bolshevism," *London Mercury,* XVII (November 1927), 52–61.

Mackiewicz, Stanislaw. *Dostoevsky.* London: Orbis, 1947.

Madaule, Jacques. "Camus et Dostoievski," *La Table Ronde,* CXLVI (February 1960), 127–136.

Malraux, André. "Author's Preface" to *Days of Wrath.* Tr. Haakon M. Chevalier. New York: Random House, 1936.

Malraux, André. "Réponse à Léon Trotsky," *La Nouvelle Revue Française,* XXXVI (April 1931), 501–507.

Maritain, Jacques. "Concerning Poetic Knowledge," in J. and R. Maritain, *The Situation of Poetry.* New York: Philosophical Library, 1955. Pp. 37–70.

Matlaw, Ralph E. "Recurrent Imagery in Dostoevskij," *Harvard Slavic Studies*, III (1957), 201–225.

Melville, Herman. "Hawthorne and His Mosses," in *Herman Melville*. Ed. Willard Thorp. New York: American Book, 1938. Pp. 327–345.

Mendilow, A. A. *Time and the Novel*. London: Peter Nevill, 1952.

Micha, René. "L'Agneau dans le placard," *La Nouvelle Nouvelle Revue Française*, XV (March 1960), 501–505.

Miller, Paul W. "Sun and Fire in Melville's *Moby-Dick*," *Nineteenth Century Fiction*, XIII (September 1958), 139–144.

Millhauser, Milton. "The Form of *Moby-Dick*," *The Journal of Aesthetics and Art Criticism*, XIII (June 1955), 527–532.

Minor, Anne. "The Short Stories of Albert Camus," *Yale French Studies*, XXV (1960), 75–80.

Moser, Charles A. *Antinihilism in the Russian Novel in the 1860's*. The Hague: Mouton, 1964.

Motchoulski, Constantin [K. V. Mochulskit]. *Dostoievski, L'homme et l'oeuvre*. Tr. G. Welter. Paris: Payot, 1963.

Mueller, William R. *The Prophetic Voice in Modern Fiction*. New York: Association Press, 1959.

Mumford, Lewis. *Herman Melville*. New York: Harcourt, Brace, 1929.

Murray, Henry A. "In Nomine Diaboli," in Tyrus Hillway and Luther S. Mansfield, eds., *Moby-Dick Centennial Essays*. Dallas: Southern Methodist University Press, 1953. Pp. 3–21.

Myers, Henry A. "Captain Ahab's Discovery: The Tragic Meaning of *Moby-Dick*," *New England Quarterly*, XV (March 1942), 15–34.

Nicolas, André. *Une Philosophie de l'existence: Albert Camus*. Paris: Presses Universitaires de France, 1964.

Olson, Charles. *Call Me Ishmael*. New York: Reynal and Hitchcock, 1947.

Olson, Charles. "Melville et Shakespeare, ou la découverte de *Moby-Dick*," *Les Temps Modernes*, VII (October 1951), 647–676.

Otto, Rudolf. *Das Heilige; über das Irrationale in der Idee des Göttlichen und sein Verhältnis zum Rationalen*. Breslau: Trewendt und Granier, 1917.

Payne, Robert. *Dostoyevsky: A Human Portrait*. New York: Alfred Knopf, 1961.

Percival, M. O. *A Reading of Moby-Dick*. Chicago: University of Chicago Press, 1950.

Poggioli, Renato. "Dostoevski, or Reality and Myth," in *The Phoenix and the Spider*. Cambridge: Harvard University Press, 1957. Pp. 16–32.

Pommer, Henry F. *Milton and Melville*. Pittsburgh: University of Pittsburgh Press, 1950.

Praz, Mario. *The Romantic Agony*. Tr. Angus Davidson. New York: World Publishing, 1956.

Rahv, Philip. "Dostoevski and Politics: Notes on *The Possessed*," *Partisan Review*, V (July 1938), 25–36.

Ramsey, Paul. "God's Grace and Man's Guilt," *Journal of Religion*, XXXI (January 1951), 21–37.

Ramsey, Warren. "Albert Camus on Capital Punishment: His Adaptation of *The Possessed*," Yale Review, XLVIII (Summer 1959), 634–640.

Rosen, Nathan. "Chaos and Dostoevsky's Women," *Kenyon Review*, XX (Spring 1958), 257–277.

Roudiez, Leon S. "Camus and *Moby-Dick*," *Symposium*, XV (Spring 1961), 30–40.

Roudiez, Leon S. "*L'Etranger, La Chute*, and the Aesthetic Legacy of Gide," *The French Review*, XXXII (February 1959), 300–310.

Roudiez, Leon S. "Strangers in Melville and Camus," *The French Review*, XXXI (January 1958), 217–226.

Rudich, Norman. "Individual as Myth," *Chicago Review*, XIII (Summer 1959), 94–119.

Sartre, Jean-Paul. "Albert Camus," *France Observateur*, January 7, 1960, p. 17.

Schogt, H. G. *La Solitude du souterrain*. The Hague: Mouton, 1958.

Sealts, Merton M. *Melville's Reading: A Check-list of Books Owned and Borrowed*. Madison: University of Wisconsin Press, 1966.

Sewall, Richard B. *The Vision of Tragedy*. New Haven: Yale University Press, 1959.

Simmons, E. J. *Dostoievsky: The Making of a Novelist*. New York: Vintage Books, 1962.

Simon, Jean. *Herman Melville, marin, métaphysicien, et poète*. Paris: Boivin, 1939.

Steiner, George. *Tolstoy or Dostoevsky*. New York: Vintage Books, 1961.

Stourzh, Gerald. "The Unforgivable Sin: An Interpretation of *The Fall*," *Chicago Review*, XV (Summer 1961), 45–57.

Strem, George C. "The Moral World of Dostoevsky," *Russian Review*, XVI (July 1957), 15–26.

Sühnel, Rudolf. "Melvilles *Moby-Dick*: Versuch einer Deutung," *Die Neuere Sprachen*, V (1956), 553–562.

Theis, R. "Albert Camus' Rückkehr zu Sisyphus," *Romanische Forschungen*, LXX (1958), 66–90.

Thompson, Lawrance. *Melville's Quarrel with God*. Princeton: Princeton University Press, 1952.

Tillich, Paul. "Protestantism and Artistic Style," in *The Theology of Culture*. New York: Oxford University Press, 1959. Pp. 68–75.

Toenes, Sara. "Public Confession in *La Chute*," *Wisconsin Studies in Contemporary Literature*, IV (Autumn 1963), 305–318.

Troyat, Henri. *Dostoievsky*. Paris: Librairie Arthème Fayard, 1940.

Ullmann, Stephen. "The Two Styles of Camus," in *The Image in the Modern French Novel*. Cambridge, England: The University Press, 1960. Pp. 239–299.

Valéry, Paul. "Autour de Corot," in *Pièces sur l'art*. Paris: Editions de la *NRF*, 1938. Pp. 135–159.

Valéry, Paul. *Introduction to the Method of Leonardo da Vinci*. Tr. T. McGreevy. London: John Rodker, 1929.

Viggiani, Carl A. "Camus and the Fall from Innocence," *Yale French Studies*, XXV (1960), 65–71.

Vincent, Howard P. *The Trying-out of Moby-Dick*. Boston: Houghton Mifflin, 1949.

Vogel, Dan. "The Dramatic Chapters in *Moby-Dick*," *Nineteenth Century Fiction*, XIII (December 1958), 239–247.

Vot, André Le. "Shakespeare et Melville: Le Thème impérial dans *Moby-Dick*," *Etudes Anglaises*, XVII (October-December 1964), 549–563.

Walcutt, Charles C. "The Fire Symbolism in *Moby-Dick*," *Modern Language Notes*, LIX (April 1944), 304–310.

Waldberg, Patrick. *Surrealism*. New York: McGraw-Hill, 1965.

Weltsch, Felix. *Religion und Humor im Leben und Werk Franz Kafkas*. Berlin: F. A. Herbig, 1957.

Yarmolinsky, Avraham. *Dostoevsky, His Life and Art*. 2nd ed., revised and enlarged. New York: Criterion Books, 1957.

Young, James D. "The Nine Gams of the 'Pequod,'" *American Literature*, XXV (January 1954), 449–463.

Zander, Leon A. *Dostoevsky*. Tr. Natalie Duddington. London: SCM Press, 1948.

Index

DATE DUE			
FEB 17 1989			

17322   808.33
                               Rys

Rysten

False prophets